SUSPENDING DISBELIEF

In memory of Joan Littlewood

SUSPENDING DISBELIEF

Theatre as Context for Sharing

ROGER GRAINGER

sussex
ACADEMIC
PRESS
Brighton • Portland • Toronto

2 4 6 8 10 9 7 5 3 1

First published in 2010 by
SUSSEX ACADEMIC PRESS
PO Box 139
Eastbourne BN24 9BP

and in the United States of America by
SUSSEX ACADEMIC PRESS
920 NE 58th Ave   Suite 300
Portland, Oregon 97213-3786

and in Canada by
SUSSEX ACADEMIC PRESS (CANADA)
90 Arnold Avenue, Thornhill, Ontario L4J 1B5

Personal names throughout the book have been changed.

British Library Cataloguing in Publication Data
A CIP catalogue record for this book is available from the British Library.

Library of Congress Cataloging-in-Publication Data
Grainger, Roger.
Suspending disbelief : theatre as context for sharing / Roger Grainger.
p. cm.
Includes bibliographical references and index.
ISBN 978-1-84519-398-0 (pbk. : alk. paper)
  1. Theater—Psychological aspects. 2. Emotions. 3. Sharing.
4. Theater audiences. 5. Theater—Philosophy. 6. Theater and society. 7. Drama—Therapeutic use. I. Title.
PN2049.G72 2010
792.01'9—dc22

2009050512

Mixed Sources
Product group from well-managed forests and other controlled sources
www.fsc.org Cert no. SGS-COC-2482
© 1996 Forest Stewardship Council
FSC

Typeset and designed by SAP, Brighton & Eastbourne
Printed by TJ International, Padstow, Cornwall.
This book is printed on acid-free paper.

CONTENTS

FOREWORD BY
BARBARA JEFFORD

Human beings seem to be obsessed by the need to be a part of some larger whole; a team, a club, a crowd, a mob, a congregation or an audience. It is this last manifestation, that of audience, or, more particularly, audience to drama, that Roger Grainger deals with so intriguingly in this important book. He writes from the point of view of someone who has been involved in the world of drama as an actor as well as a skilled academic observer; a dual function I cannot share with him, although I have a lifetime of experience as a performer. This performing experience enables me to recognise the role that an audience plays in the presentation of a drama. This may seem strange, surely the presence of an audience is essential to the performance of a play? Well, no! There is always one 'run through' of a play in the last days of rehearsal that seems to capture the intentions of the author in the clearest way, it becomes a sort of template for the re-creation of that closeness through hundreds of performances in the presence of that last member of the cast to arrive, the audience. The audience is evaluated and commented on by the performers: 'They're good tonight!' 'Nice house!', 'a bit sticky!' – the drama is indeed, as Roger Grainger says, a 'context for sharing'; sharing, that basic desire to become part of a larger whole. By indulging that desire through the world of drama, people are able to make a positive contribution to the presentation of a work of art, to join with the author's interpreters on stage and their fellow audience members in that intoxicating 'suspension of disbelief' that is such an integral part of a memorable stage performance, Roger Grainger leads us through this process with great insight. I enjoyed taking the journey with him, as I am sure you will.

PREFACE AND ACKNOWLEDGEMENTS

This book owes its existence to four people.

I am indebted to Barbara Jefford and Siân Phillips for allowing me to include their perceptive Foreword and Postscript. The *Everyman Companion to Shakespeare* (ed. Gareth and Barbara Lloyd Evans, London: Dent, 1985) describes Barbara as "an actress of powerful address, whose Cleopatra and Lady Macbeth rank among the finest of the post-war era". For me. she will always be St. Joan, and I was honoured to be a fellow member of the cast of Shaw's play, which the Old Vic took to the Moscow Arts Theatre in 1961. (I was in Macbeth, too, but unfortunately missed Cleopatra . . .) Sincere gratitude to a great artist, who was the youngest ever recipient of the OBE for her services to the theatre.

Siân too has played St. Joan, to critical acclaim. She has been a central figure within British theatre for many years now, and has made a succession of films and television programmes, one of her most celebrated roles being that of Livia in the classic BBC series *I Claudius*. Her one-woman cabaret show, 'Marlene', based on the work of Marlene Dietrich, revealed her amazing versatility and won her a 'Tony' nomination. In June 2000, Siân was awarded a CBE in the Queen's Birthday Honours list. Her television roles have always given much joy to a very great number of people – but I remember her best for the parts she played when we were fellow students at RADA.

The third person I would like to thank died some years ago: Joan Littlewood, to whom this book is dedicated. In my view Joan was a genius, the only one I have ever known, and she it was who taught me how theatre works. The first time I played at the Moscow Arts Theatre, it was in her company.

My wife, Doreen, is a fellow actor (as well as a patient proof-reader). It is largely through her that I have maintained a living involvement in theatre, and I offer her my sincere thanks

Suspending Disbelief

CHAPTER ONE
LEARNING

Watching cats puts me in mind of Thorndike. E.L. Thorndike was a psychologist who put his cat in a box to see if it could get out. There was only one way out of the box and it took the cat some time and a good deal of effort to find it, and when it did it was by mistake. (He backed up against the lever!). The point is, however, that every time the psychologist put his cat in his puzzle-box, the cat went through everything he had done before in order to get to the point at which he could jump out, purring, and proceed to rub himself against Thorndike's leg.[1]

It was a good game and he learned it quickly: all of it. The game was getting out of the box, and you had to do it properly, the way you had learned it, or it wouldn't work. No-one – particularly a psychologist like Thorndike – is suggesting here that the cat had done what we would do. At no point did the cat stand back and think about the situation. If he had done, he could have made the appropriate (humanly appropriate, that is) adjustments to his behaviour and got out very much sooner. Nor is it likely that he thought, as we might have done, this is a game and I must play it properly or it won't be any fun. He simply carried out a sequence of behaviours which he discovered to be satisfactory.

Cats don't analyse. They keep to patterns of behaviour which have worked in the past, until they back into a short-cut which is able to give a more immediate result and start doing this instead. In psychologese, their 'goal-directed behaviour consists of 'action pathways' which are not distinguished from the goal itself because they are both learned together. Or so it seems.

To a large extent this is how it seems with human beings too. For example, I never intended to spend this much time writing about cats in a book about theatre; but one thing led to another, and cats seemed a good place to start, for their own sake certainly, but mainly because of where they will lead. Where things lead is a principal preoccupation for human beings as well as for cats. We, too, carry out the business of living in sequence; a succession of beginnings and endings which we endeavour to arrange in a purposeful relationship to each other, so that each beginning will lead to the end which we have chosen for it, thus succeeding in whatever it may be that we have set out to do. As we have seen, we are able to plan these things in advance and to adjust our plans before they have any chance of failure or success; we can envisage a range of action pathways without actually having to try any of them out. The capability to 'look before we leap' in this way is something we do not have to think about. Unless we are philosophers we simply take it for granted. It might be pointed out even at this early stage in my argument (or hypothetical action plan) that the ease with which we are able to substitute thinking about doing something for actually doing it does not necessarily always contribute to a satisfactory – *i.e.* enjoyable – outcome.[2]

Thinking about how we behave leads inevitably into considering how we relate to other people, which means how we communicate with them, both directly using our senses to transmit our meanings and intentions to other people (and animals), and indirectly, giving them the responsibility to interpret our behaviour, sometimes as they themselves think fit, but more often as we set out to manipulate them into doing, along the lines of actions speaking louder than words. Here again, the notion of a meaningful *sequence* of events prevails, as words are organised into sentences and sentences become paragraphs and so on up to the book's last page. Not only verbal communication follows this rule. Our gestures, if they are to be properly expressive, happen in a succession of moves each contributing to the meaning of what we are setting out to express – thus we smile, stand, lift up our hands and cheer, or scowl, turn our shoulder, bend our arm and shake our fist. It takes all of the sequence to make a single point.

And this *is* the point, that the sentence, the book, the gesture are unitary. Each makes a statement distinguishing itself from others which could be made. They are all put together out of various behavioural elements to deliver one message, speak with one voice. Their message may be complicated, may in fact consist of many messages, but their delivering it together, in unison, remains the principal thing transmitted – this is what is meant and the way in which it is meant – which may itself *be* the point.

Bateson calls this the 'meta-message', which means the one embodied in the way we have chosen to deliver it. The marvellous freedom to experience, and to experience ourselves doing so, involves us in the possibility of choosing whether we will reveal or disguise our intentions towards one another. In terms of meanings we intend to communicate, we can behave well or badly, straightforwardly or deviously, honestly or dishonestly. We can say what we want others to think we mean . . . [3]

But all this has to be spelled out. None of it is instantaneous or unitary. After all it is communication, a way of pulling things together. We can reserve our actual meanings and substitute others to do their work in the interchange of ideas and feelings, gesture and response which communicate our experiences of ourselves and others; which means we can say what we partly mean without actually having to lie.

This is all very natural to us; so natural in fact that we do it without thinking, certainly without any real intention to deceive. After all, it wouldn't do to let everybody know everything about us, would it? It would certainly be very dangerous. A sense of our own vulnerability makes us choose what we wish to reveal and what we prefer to keep hidden.

Erving Goffman [4] called this 'impression management'. In his book *The Presentation of Self in Everyday Life* he examines ways in which, as part of our normal everyday behaviour, we arrange the way we adjust our way of putting things in line with the impression we want to make on someone else. We have the ability to tailor our messages in accordance with what we perceive to be the particular situation. This may or may not mean holding things back. If it does then there may be any number of reasons for doing this, only some of them excuses for the times when we are deceiving the other – or the others – in order to protect ourselves against their finding out what we really think or feel about things and arriving at a more accurate assessment of the kind of people we are, or think we are. Goffman uses a theatrical metaphor in order to get his message across, distinguishing between experience we wish to communicate to others, the self we put on show, and that which we see ourselves as needing to keep to ourselves. The difference is clearly recognisable in social life, where so many of the things we set out to do together correspond to this division between 'back-stage' and 'on-stage' (and its variations such as 'up stage' and 'down stage', where the former stage position inevitably focuses more of the audience's attention than the latter, simply because action taking place there is further away, so that we need to concentrate all the harder.) Goffman points out that social institutions inevitably require people cast as either 'insiders' or 'outsiders', those 'running the show' and the rest of society, all of which is to a greater or lesser degree 'on the outside', however closely associated its members may be with its particular purpose or function. This division is clearly expressed in our current ways of talking about the various social agencies we come into contact with, dividing ourselves up into 'users' and 'providers' of services, the latter functioning 'back stage'. (When they do appear, of course, it is usually 'up stage'.)

Goffman talks about *tropes*,[5] which is another word for metaphors of a dramatic kind: sequences of events transmitting meaning indirectly rather than in so many words. We 'get the picture' because of what happens in the mini-dramas we present to one another and the world. An example of this would be for somebody to say, "So I turned right to them and I said . . . " The picture presented here is of one person turning dramatically to another person in order to say something they think that person ought to hear. In fact, however, no such actual scenario took place. The 'turning' is a figure of speech, a trope. We dramatise things in this way simply to make the account more vivid. There is no intention to lie or to distort truth in any way. Quite the opposite; for this is the way we have at our disposal to bring home the truth as we ourselves have experienced it, and this, so far as we are concerned, is as honest as we can possibly get.

This is our wonderful freedom as human beings, the ability to look both at and through, to accept and to interpret; to encode our messages one way and communicate their actual meaning in another. Its usefulness as a way of hiding the truth from other people and ourselves is glaringly obvious. It is, however, the way our minds work. We may strive for 'real' honesty, for a total transparency of thought and action, avoiding anything which could be taken as the implication of an implication. We can certainly aim for such single-mindedness; but it wouldn't be honesty we were aiming for, but the triumph of our powers of self-deception.

If by some chance we managed to bring such a thing off, it would make us less than human. Using one part of ourselves to check up on another part, one mental faculty to monitor another is the way we function as human beings. It is our human-ness.[6] We use it all the time, not in an unbroken stream of double awareness but backwards and forwards, like the ticking of a clock. We use it for honesty as well as concealment, to carry out our purpose to make real contact with other people, to tell ourselves that this is what we are doing, that it represents a real intention to 'come clean' and not hold back – because this is something which, after all, we, as well as they, need to know.

Looking at them, we look at ourselves too, seeing ourselves involved in the business of working together, us with them and them with us, as we re-discover ourselves in the action of sharing. When we are together in this way our personhood, our individual self, expands. We remain ourselves but we agree with others. (If this is what we choose to do, of course. As Samuel Butler says[7], "He who complies against his will, Is of the same opinion still.") Sincere agreement makes us that much surer of ourselves, even though we may be aware that it constitutes a certain surrender of our autonomy. The fact is, we need the support of others, so if it is a surrender it is a willing one.

Involvement and withdrawal are movements of the soul. They express human, personal intention at its most fundamental level. In a sense they are the same movement as it takes place in opposing directions. When we join up with others intending to co-operate with them we move into a new dimension, one of encounters that are shared. We agree to do things together, and this necessitates a change in the way we think about things too. On this new plane we will be moving in unison. This, at least, is our intention. We are still free to look at ourselves from our own point of view, commenting on what is happening in our own private way, drawing our own conclusions. However, we are aware that, with this proviso, sharing is actually in our best interests.

This, of course, is the principle which underlies our social life, the decision to relinquish our autonomy, in all its vulnerability, in exchange for the strength and confidence we call corporate, involving an agreement to do things together and do them in a particular way – the first for strength, the second for safety, although in practice the two reinforce each other. Working together makes us more efficient and it usually happens for entirely functional purposes, as a way of dealing with tasks of a practical kind which are beyond the reach of individuals. Very often, however, it is done for its own sake, for the joy which comes from achieving things together as a partnership or a group of people, loosening our hold on whatever divides us and throwing ourselves into whatever it may be that we share; which turns out to be our human-ness.

When we talk about this – interacting for its own sake – we call it playing. We can, of course, play by ourselves if we have the imagination to do so, but only if we give our imaginary playmates lives of their own. Children's games in playgrounds, cup finals at Wembley, chess championships all constitute the joint decision to move away from privacy into a shared terrain and enjoy the life which lives in interchange, where things are done in the name and for the sake of doing them together – a privileged way of existing whose holiness is only really acknowledged in religious rituals throughout the world, but which occurs everywhere else in games and ceremonies that turn out to be, because of the intensity of the sharing which they embody, implicitly religious. Theatre is a case in point.

At times like this we move onto higher ground. We do so not in spite of our separate identities, but because of them. Because they are there, and ours, the urge to overcome their limitations draws us together in search of a sense of wholeness which is both special and ordinary – ordinary because it lies always within our grasp; special because however we search, we can never manage to find it anywhere else.

Theatre, too, is an agreement to adopt this special sharing

mode. In theatre we move into a place set apart for the sharing of imagination. Like other games, theatre is formative of a particular state of mind. It is a way in which we learn to live as human beings, as Thorndike's box helped his cat overcome the difficulties involved in life as a domestic animal. Because we are concerned here with people rather than animals, questions are bound to arise concerning the truth or otherwise of our intentions. The honesty of theatre consists in the agreement to share an imaginative action. So long as the operation remains within this particular realm, that of shared imagination rather than private fantasy it is considered to be, and experienced as, emotionally and cognitively safe. That is, it will not intrude upon our privacy unless we invite it in.

Psychologically speaking the action of inviting people into our private world, their presence in that world, presents certain problems to us. This is true however psychologically stable we may consider ourselves to be, however safe we like to think we are 'in ourselves'. R. D. Laing's[8] interpersonal analysis of mental health distinguishes three directions from which our peace of mind may be disturbed with regard to the presence, or even the existence, of the other people who make up our world. The first of these is the danger of their taking us over in a way which could cancel us out and reduce us to a condition in which our individual identity would be subsumed in theirs. Laing calls this fear of 'engulfment', and points out that it is particularly threatening because of its ability to pose as love – "To be hated may be feared for other reasons, but to be hated as such is often less disturbing than to be destroyed, as it is felt, through being engulfed by love" (1959, p. 43)[9]

This fear of being taken over which, says Laing, we all fear to some degree, is greatly reduced by a situation in which we agree to share our vulnerability, admitting at the same time that we may be called on to live through situations, actual or imagined, we would rather not face alone, without an agreement to share the load. The second of Laing's sources of interpersonal threat is 'implosion', the terrifying experience of immobility, when time has stopped and we lose the ability to move out of an experience which, though intolerable, must still be tolerated. At such times, it is as if the roof of our world has crashed in on us, trapping us under its weight. Although this seems an abnormal occurrence, much too dramatic to be part of ordinary human experience, it is one which is really extremely near the surface. As the survivor of a car accident said to me, "Once the clock has been stopped it seems impossible to get it started again." It can take something considerably less than this to 'stop us dead in our tracks'. The same devastating effect may be caused by the sudden, unforeseen end of a relationship.

The third anxiety mentioned is 'petrification', being reduced to what Laing describes as "an *it* without subjectivity" (p.46). Like the other two it describes a way in which we interact with our empowerment of people and things which remind us of them. In this case it usually reflects someone else's defensiveness, a situation or occasion when they feel threatened by our own presence as people and consequently take steps to de-personalise us. From this point of view it reveals itself as being intentional in a way that 'engulfment' and 'implosion' are not. All the same it works in the same subliminal way on people's states of mind, and needs the same sensitivity on the part of all of us to the things which affect the quality of our relationships with others.

Theatre cuts across these sources of human distress, each of which refers to situations in which we confront and are confronted by others. These are the things which we fear may happen when we 'come up against' people. The agreement to share is intended to remove the threat of things like this. From now on we will all be 'facing in the same direction', regarding one another as fellow human beings rather than rivals who must compete with one another for their own emotional survival.

At the very heart of theatre is the agreement to share. So much is obvious. Plays, like other games, depend on co-operation, the decision taken by a group of people, that they will have a shared purpose. This may involve conflict, but this will be strictly regulated and end in being resolved in a way which fulfils the original intention, which was not in fact to win but simply to play this particular game. The game of theatre is, as we have seen, a special one. It is a game of believing about things in a particular way, or looking at truth from a certain angle. You may or may not succeed in doing this, but the game is to try to do it; for in its basic form it is the most authentically human type of social interaction of all.

CHAPTER TWO

TRUSTING

In art we share the truth conveying game of imagination. This is how the author of *The Rime of the Ancient Mariner* describes the way imagination works:

> This power . . . reveals itself in the balance or reconcilement of opposite or discordant qualities; of sameness with difference; of the general with the concrete; the idea with the image; the individual with the representative; the sense of novelty and freshness with old and familiar objects; a more than usual state of emotion with a more than usual order; judgement ever awake and steady with enthusiasm and feeling, profound or vehement; and while it blends and harmonises the natural and artificial, still subordinates art to nature.[10]

Poets, says Coleridge, use imagination as a way of bringing reconciliation to a world at odds with itself. Poetry's job is to heal divisions and bridge gaps within our human perception of reality. Occasions which bring people together for a single shared purpose obviously work in this direction; but poetry expresses the heart of the impulse to share experiences which normally divide us.

Not automatically, however. We have to agree to the process. We ourselves must choose to change our minds about reality, what may or may not be believed, and adopt a way of thinking and feeling, a way of *behaving*, which is able to transcend, for a short time at least, the discords which are so much a part of our common experience, 'life in the real world'. We do not have to be mystics to do this, nor do we have to be poetic geniuses like Coleridge. We simply have to use our imaginations in a particular way – one involving a willingness to realise the world we are bringing into existence by undertaking to believe in one another's visions.

This, then, is "that willing suspension of disbelief for the moment which constitutes poetic faith" (ch.14). Coleridge's well-known phrase refers to every kind of poetic experience. Whether the expressive medium is aural, visual or tactile, we must be willing to allow it to be, for us, something very different from what it is, while of course giving it permission to remain itself. We must be willing, when we are invited, to look through and beyond the factual reality of words, textures, shapes, movements, gestures, to the meaning they are intended to convey.

For meaning, read organisation: the arrangement of parts into recognisable wholes, ideas and experiences we can assimilate, feelings we can share. The most poetic experience of all is recognition of an emotion that is shared, a picture which touches the imagination of everyone who stops and stands in order to have a better look, a piece of music which moves a concert hall full of individual music lovers. Or, of course, the special arrangement of events which we call a story; or rather, which we agree to regard as a story, for there must be no element of force involved. "Let me tell you a story," someone says; and we know immediately that our co-operation is called for. We ourselves must wish to transform a record of events which never took place, delivered by someone whose intention is to deceive us unto thinking that they did, happening to people who, as the storyteller is perfectly aware, never actually existed at all, into something which in some way or other may affect the way we think and feel about ourselves and our relationship with the world we live in.[11]

All this is of fundamental importance for the way we grow as people. This being the case, we are exceedingly blessed in the ease with which it actually happens! The imagination involved is something we already possess. What we have to do it allow ourselves to say Yes – and even this is much easier to do when there is more than one person at a time doing it. Herein lies the transformative effect of theatre. Theatre is a corporate experience of poetry. Aristotle, like Coleridge, sees poetry as essentially a healing experience, one in which the painful lesions of human awareness caused by our inability to reconcile 'things which don't fit', wounds made worse by our attempts to hide them from sight, are eased by allowing ourselves to be involved in a story in which we are able to share the experience of being human. Aristotle's theory of catharsis[12] uses drama as an illustration of a principle which lies at the heart of all poetry; that of discovering oneself in the action of losing oneself. Certainly this is a very familiar idea, if not an actual cliché. We talk of 'losing ourselves' in the fictional world of a book or a film, or of having our imagination seized by a poet's use of language, words which have

> Charm'd magic casements, opening on the foam
> Of perilous seas, in faery lands forlorn.
>
> (KEATS, *Ode to a Nightingale*)

Aristotle means more than this, however. In drama, as he describes it, our involvement goes deeper. We are healed 'by pity and fear' not simply by imagination: the pity and fear we ourselves feel owing to our personal concern for the characters in the play. Our world is implied by theirs because we ourselves are implicated in their experience. Aristotle describes the emotionally liberating effect of allowing ourselves to be imaginatively led into intimate contact with people and situations which appear at first sight not to be our concern, only to discover that this is far from the case. The word 'empathy' was not current in Aristotle's day, but what he is suggesting is precisely this. In theatre we are drawn into people's lives because we have embraced the opportunity of temporarily making their world our own. The situation is a fictional one; the people concerned have no life other than the one they share with us. We choose to avoid the labour involved in dealing with the things which happen to us in the world we normally inhabit by giving reality, our own personal reality, to one in which the destiny of all involved has already been decided, choosing in fact not to choose at all, but simply respond to what our heart is telling us. Our intellect assures us that it is safe to do so, that there is simply no reason to take these things seriously, as if they had any real relevance with regard to our own lives. However our emotions choose not to listen, preferring to suffer and to triumph with the people in the play. It isn't actually me, we say, but it *could* be, couldn't it?

In fact, it isn't. However in imagination it may very well be, because in our own emotional experience and that of the man or woman sitting next to us, this is something which has already happened. We have been here before. At this point we may very well ask ourselves why we came. What on earth were we thinking of? Whatever it was, it certainly wasn't *this*; quite the opposite in fact, because 'this' is precisely what we spend a lot of time not thinking about. Whatever it was, it was an occasion of some pain for us and our efforts to 'forget it and move on' – as we are always being told we should do – have left us vulnerable to anything which reminds us of it. So – why *did* we come?

In Aristotle's famous phrase, we came to be "purged". In theatre we bring hidden things into the light of day, to the surface of our minds and allow ourselves the chance to deal with them properly, which means to suffer on account of them. Theatres are places for laying ghosts. As it turns out, the common sense which has prompted us to try and forget, now allows us to find a way of remembering. It's only a play, we tell ourselves; no need to take it seriously and allow ourselves to be upset about what is going on in front of us. After all, we've been to plays before, and we tell ourselves we've benefited from the experience too. It's only a play, so why not relax, forget our stupid fears and join in with whatever may be going on.

Which, of course, is what we do. We certainly benefit from the experience, because becoming involved in another person's life has the effect of making us more conscious of our own reality, and if we can manage to allow ourselves to do this without feeling a need to defend ourselves against it, if for a time at least we can be less self-conscious, more other-aware, then the burden of having to acknowledge our own pain is eased by the deeply human satisfaction of sharing. The terms on which we share are revealed as less important, less divisive, than the fact of our sharing. If we are willing to allow ourselves to participate in another's pain we may discover who we are and that our belonging together is the most vital thing about us – that it is, in fact, our reality.

Not that we think it is. Neither in the theatre nor in our daily life do we really believe that the way we find ourselves is by giving ourselves away. Christians may accept the idea because they have been told to do by the Son of God; but that remains a matter of faith and therefore, by definition, impractical. However all the same, it happens. We seldom enquire how it does so, because it is so natural to us, so spontaneous, that we take it for granted, this marvellous interchange of separate existences which characterises us as people rather than any other form of natural – or artificial – life. We make use of it all the time, for liberation or control, for the encounter itself exerts no force at all over what we may decide to do with it.

So natural is this empathetic unity of feeling that we scarcely notice it. The way we work is the way we work, and when we think about it we become self-conscious and so miss the point – which is a presence, not an idea, just as if we try to think about someone without actually imagining them, we find it impossible to do. Imagination turns out to be the enabling factor in the dynamic of personal relationship; and it is something which easily escapes our own attempts to tie it down. Its essence is perceptual freedom and that is how we experience it, left to ourselves.

Some things do not 'leave us to ourselves', however. Poetry is one of these and drama is another. Theatre in particular is a mechanism for harnessing the imagination, directing individual imaginations to where they belong – in a creative interchange of personal meanings, human presences. Look at it this way, the theatre building is a metaphor for another kind of structure altogether, erected as a container for the impulse to explore the essence of human-ness – what we and other people mean to one another, how we belong together, and how difficult and painful, as well as joyful and rewarding, this belonging inevitably turns out to be.

"The balance or reconcilement of opposite or discordant qualities" giving rise to "a more than usual state of emotion with a more than usual order." Coleridge agrees with Aristotle about the need for opposites to find some way in which they can be brought together. They recognise poetry as the way this can be done, the element capable of synthesising the contrary emotions of fear and pity which, deep within the human breast, continue to struggle with each other. Aristotle, in particular, focuses upon theatre as the most striking expression of this battle between emotions. The theatres which he himself knew demonstrated, in the way they were constructed, what Martin Buber describes as "the stern over-againstness of I and Thou".[13] It is not only a function of Greek theatre, where stage and auditorium were separated by many feet of empty space. Everywhere where theatre takes place – on television, video or radio, or on the cinema screen – the separation asserts itself, so that between those telling the story and those being drawn into it, there is a space which must be crossed. Crossing such a divide requires no effort. All it requires is willingness to 'play the game'. A careful balance between safety and danger in which we can forget our fears in reaching out, reaching *across*.

The feelings which disturb us so much that we regard them as too dangerous to be contemplated are always basically about people. Drama presents these feelings to us as personages in a play. We may identify ourselves with them in their personified form, the guise they adopt as actual characters in an imaginary scenario, or we may keep them at a distance, at arms' length, where they are very much easier to live with – being, after all, only imaginary constructs. In the terms set out in Aristotle's *Poetics* we may pity these ghostly presences who remind us so much of ourselves, and endow them with an immediacy which belongs to us – thus, in Coleridge's phrase, 'believing' in them, or we can allow our fear of the feelings which they embody to remind us that, after all, this is only a game, a party trick dreamed up for our amusement, so that we can play at feelings without having to pay the prices attached to them 'in the real world'. How deeply we choose to identify with the play is always, in the last resort, our own concern. It is up to us whether we let ourselves be *exposed* to our fears – including our fears of other people – or merely *distracted* from them, according to the measure of our willingness to become imaginatively involved.

There is a third option, however, which depends on theatre's ability to let us do both these things, preserving a balance between them, allowing us to live with our powerful emotions and not be overcome by them. What Coleridge says about the power of poetry to reconcile opposites is demonstrated more clearly here than anywhere else, in the state of emotional equilibrium we identify as catharsis. Here, in the shared atmosphere of the theatrical event we enjoy both tension and release, the result being "A more than usual state of emotion" combined with "a more than usual order."[14]

Many psychotherapists work on the principle that emotional healing requires not the suppression of emotion but its integration with awareness. This, however, cannot be forced; a way has to be found of releasing it so that it begins to form part of a way of regarding our story about ourselves rather than an unthinkable gap we have had to leave in it. The agreement to suspend disbelief can only take place when there is a willingness for it to do so; and this means that we must feel safe enough to move emotionally in a direction which at one and the same time alarms and attracts us, causing a psychological impasse in which our ordinary ways of coping no longer work for us and we throw ourselves into the creation of something else, some*where* else. Faced with the radical need for poetry, we give shape to a world where wounds are healed and our deepest longings satisfied.

Writing about catharsis, Thomas Scheff[15] explains how:

> When we cry over the fate of Romeo and Juliet, we are reliving our own personal experiences of overwhelming loss, but under new and less severe conditions. (1979, p. 13)

These conditions are in fact the recognition of the fact that the need for our fears to be expressed, so that in some way they can be laid to rest, is not ours alone but is shared by others who have an answering fear of rejection and need for reassurance. Our tears express our experience of release, the deep joy which floods through us when we no longer have to pretend not to feel, not to care. Certainly we have permitted ourselves to care for others, but at the expense of not allowing ourselves to care for ourselves. The emotion of caring, of allowing ourselves to share another's burden even in imagination, is a positive one, able to balance the negativity represented by our fearfulness, if we can find a way of realising it and putting it to work, for the good of everyone involved and our own peace of mind.

'Even in imagination'; but it is imagination which is crucial and through it we make sense of the business of living together, relating what we know is happening to us to what we imagine is happening to them. Intuition, insight, empathy are all words for imagination. Without our fears we could not care, except for ourselves – which, of course, is another way of saying that we would cease to be human beings. We cannot simply cancel our fears out; we have to use our imagination to find a way of neutralising their control over us, balancing our fear of being left unprotected – always something we can easily imagine – with our ability to involve ourselves in the needs of others, which is likewise a product of imagination on our part.

In the world of imaginative sharing, the shared world of poetry which uses various forms of art to communicate its meanings, self and other meet as both different and the same, separate and yet united. This is symbolised by the existence, whether visible or invisible, of a space 'between' specially provided to pay due respect for our need to remain safely 'in' ourselves. The *reason* for this separation is human emotional self-protectiveness: it is there so that we may feel safe. Its purpose, however, is entirely the opposite, because it provides us with what we need in order to put ourselves in the very danger we fear, which is that we should somehow become involved with whatever happens 'on the other side'. The barrier beckons as powerfully as it discourages. Its presence challenges our imagination, a faculty over which we have little, if any, control. We are willing to take the chance of following where it leads us even if this means becoming emotionally involved with the world existing on the other side of the specially contrived 'distancing' effect. Encouraged by imagination, we balance the odds and arrive at a decision to move onto higher ground.

> At aesthetic distance the members of the audience become emotionally involved in the drama, but not to the point where they forget that they are also observers. Aesthetic distance may be defined as the simultaneous and equal experience of being both participant and observer.[16]

Scheff describes the balance between safety and danger on

which our willingness to 'join the story' depends. If we refuse to allow our imagination to work this commonplace conjuring trick involving parallel worlds, in which the reality-bound nature of one of them tempers the other's capability of disarming human realism altogether, we exclude ourselves from an experience of sharing a truth about ourselves which our self-protectiveness so often leads us to ignore: that human life is exchanged not possessed so that our identity as persons subsists in our ability to *share*. If imagination helps us to do so, then the attitude of mind which requires us to attach a greater value to things which we can tie down, and consequently have to take charge of, than to realities which escape our intellectual grasp, is likely to prove a disadvantage.

In theatre, imagination is incarnated in the living presence of actors and audience. We are invited in by real people, sustained in their ability to tell a story by the reality bestowed on them by our participation in the world which they are creating for us. Our willingness to make their story ours as well as theirs constitutes its reality for all who take part both as actors and audiences. "Gentle breath of yours my sails Must fill," says Prospero in the epilogue to Shakespeare's *The Tempest*.[17] The action is mutual, however, as actors and audience co-operate to give themselves away to one another, and thus give life to a world which they have laboured to co-create.

The 'suspension of disbelief' cited by Coleridge is an exchange of gifts in which the gift is ourself. It is a game, not a trick; an expression of mutuality not a technique for manipulating. As such, it should involve neither domination nor the abrogation of responsiveness. Along with art in general, theatre provides a structure for freedom. Because its action subsists in the celebration of person-hood, its message is proclaimed on behalf of everyone who finds their own life in some way affected by it and willingly agrees to participate.

CHAPTER THREE

SHARING

The lights go on, the curtain – if there is one – rises. Or someone walks into a space which has obviously been kept empty, and we say "Who's that? What are they doing?" And even more urgently, "What do they want from us?" Whatever it may be that they want, we're willing to go as far as showing an interest: the ticket we have bought is the pledge of this, at least. We have purchased the right to be involved in the proceedings, whatever they turn out to be. So let's start, shall we? Who are *you*?

It is no ordinary ticket that we have bought. As the song says, it is "a ticket to ride". At present there doesn't seem anything to ride on except a solitary actor in a space which is conspicuously empty.[18] That, however, is the point which is being made; that the message of theatre is for us to 'watch this space'. Suspension of disbelief on our part is willing, certainly; but it is also purposeful and consequently focused. The basic mechanism of theatrical presentation consists of the purposeful arrangement of human contexts – ideas, feelings, images, sensations, present disposi- tions and historical circumstances – for the promotion of human encounter. Its contrived nature lies in arranging all these elements so that they may be presented as a single event and be received as such, in contrast to the way we experience them outside the theatre. Plays may be discursive, even expansive, but within limits.

Like other animals – including cats – we learn by doing. For us 'doing' means 'living through', in awareness of ourselves as immersed in the learning process, we see ourselves 'living and learning'. Even this is misleading, however, because so much of our human learning is not consciously registered as such; not at the time, that is. The things we really need to know are learned by immersion in life, although they are transformed into what we recognise as knowledge when we are in a position to sit back and consider what has been happening to us, what we have been thinking and feeling, and what it all meant. We draw conclusions and store them away in what psychologists often refer to as our 'memory bank'. This is the part of our mind where, intentionally or not, we keep hold on past experiences; and where these experiences work to influence the way we think and feel now. Looked at like this, we are always, as the Danish philosopher Søren Kierkegaard pointed out, a step behind ourselves, living in the past and understanding in the future.[19]

Experiences which are to be treasured are recorded in a special way, however. The vividness and immediacy we reached out for, trying hard to recapture it as we lived and felt it at the time when it was happening, rather than as it exists now, its condition compromised by everything which has taken place since as well as our memories of all that happened to us before, must be reproduced in our own personal story; this original event has to be treated as a thing apart, separated from the stream of events and the kaleidoscope of images. It becomes poeticised, addressing us personally and drawing us into a world of its own, that of "emotion recollected in tranquillity".[20]

This is a world we choose to enter, to find a release from the things which crowd in upon us from our everyday lives and relieve the pressure of work in progress; not to escape from the world but to remind us of occasions when, for us, the world possessed form and meaning. We join the story which art creates for us. In so doing we refresh our own story. For a time at least we participate in a story which has shape and purpose, whose action refreshes the yearning we have for a sense of things undertaken, endured and achieved, achieved by being endured; and whose events balance one another to produce a whole which is a recognisable event within our lives.[21]

Shape, meaning, involvement. In the eminently practical business of making sense of life, the three things are interdependent. This quality of identifiability, of an experience which is not just recognised in order to be filed away with everything associated with it, but firmly grasped in order to remain recognisable, plays a crucial role. These are the experiences which actively guide our story-building, the things we consciously refer to when we pause to reflect on our lives. Normally we are so immersed in living that we have little time for reflection; often, as we saw, having difficulty in catching up with ourselves. Something must really stand out as possessing a personal significance, if it is to stop time for us and allow us to take stock of where, and who, we are.

Thou still unravish'd bride of quietness,
Thou foster-child of silence and slow time – [22]

A poet looks at a piece of pottery and is transported into a world he knows intimately, without ever having visited the place where the pot originated. Although people portrayed on the 'Grecian Urn' are only representations, in this world of imagination their life is as vivid and full of meaning as the poet's own; more so, in fact, because they are the ones who have brought him alive by sharing their reality with his own. All this happens 'outside time'. Reading it, time is suspended for us too, by the vividness of the image which Keats creates for – and with – us.

This is a striking example of the effect of distancing in art, which is not 'involvement as opposed to detachment' but the very opposite: 'involvement *because of* detachment'. The difference lies in focus, the degree of intensity with which we concentrate on what we are perceiving – our willingness to concentrate on it alone, shutting out distractions. Our attention is seized by a powerful image, powerful because it is able to penetrate to a source of awareness which feeds our understanding without being open to the ways in which we usually describe things. When we try to tie this kind of image down we inevitably find ourselves up against the problem of resemblances which are also contrasts.

We ought not to be surprised, because art aims at baffling us as much as providing us with information, refusing to say what it would csay. Art, even dramatic art, implies more than it represents. The problem with trying to bring our powers of intellectual analysis to bear on Keats's 'Grecian Urn' is not that the image is incredible, but that it is super-credible: evading our attempts to reduce it to the level of a thing among things, it reaches out to us, grabs us and takes us somewhere else. C.G. Jung would have said that it is able to do this because it functions as a psychological archetype, "one of the primordial images" which are "dominants of the collective unconscious" which "owe their power to intrigue and involve us"[23] because, in the words of Hubert and Mauss, they are "*a priori* categories of imagination". These archetypal images resonate within the unconscious mind because they put us in touch with a way of being which our intellect manages to ignore, the spiritual awareness which defies description.

Or rather, it defies ordinary description. Poetry provides it with a vehicle, using the expressiveness of carefully chosen words to point us in the direction of wordlessness – a state of mind in which we contemplate the symbol itself, able to describe its formal characteristics but baffled by our efforts to tie it down. The true poetry, however, lies precisely here, in bafflement:

Heard melodies are sweet, but those unheard
Are sweeter.[24]

And so we are led further in, delighted by the shape and surface decoration, drawn by the urn's inability to embody the reality it represents by lending it the power to make music and dance, giving it a reality which is ours. We are welcomed into a space already prepared, one which is waiting for us and will not be filled until we ourselves fill it.

This is the way in which art works, not by force but by suggestion.. When it portrays violence, it presents it rather than creating it. It is we ourselves who bring it into existence as we respond to a beckoning presence, a place for us to be, however we decide to take advantage of the invitation. The message which a work of art has for us is always one which we have our own personal reasons for responding to or ignoring as aversive or irrelevant. However once we have responded to the invitation to 'suspend our disbelief' we find ourselves, whether we are actors or audience, opened up to the entire range of emotions required by the story. The intensity with which we feel is the measure of our involvement and of theatre's ability to focus it and draw us, for the time being, ever deeper under its spell.

This being so, it can be extremely hard to detach ourselves. The more self-enclosed is the world of the play, the space we have chosen to enter, the firmer the grasp it exerts on us. Held by what is happening in the story, discovering that we have begun to take it personally, we have difficulty in dissociating from our loyalty to it. As well as the emotional ties we have formed, and contributing to them, this is a better defined, more brightly illuminated world than ours, easier to grasp; or it is more mysterious and enticing, full of beckoning shadows; or the things which happen here are unexpected and exciting; or perhaps all these factors, and others too, contribute to an effect we hesitate to spoil by the willing assertion of literal- mindedness. Looked at like this, theatre is an easily shattered illusion which we hesitate to see shattered. All the same, it is because the illusion is so potent, the picture so vivid, that we treasure it, working hard to preserve its integrity.

Needless to say, the impulse to protect an alternative world is not the only feeling that theatre produces in us; what happens in the play itself gives rise to the whole range of human emotion, including a good deal that we usually prefer to keep under wraps, safely hidden out of sight. In the long run, as we have seen, the theatrical encounter is a healing experience, but this does not mean that the process of purging is gentle, although the circumstances in which it takes place may be perceived as safe enough. Those whose lives have been drastically affected would certainly not describe it like that. For someone whose own story is dramatically changed by imaginative participation in the fictional life of a stage character the feelings aroused by the experience may be violent ones – and this too lies at the very heart of what theatre is and what it can do to – and with – us.[25]

"A real stage play," says Antonin Artaud,

> upsets the tranquillity of our senses, releases our repressed subconscious, drives us to a kind of potential rebellion (since it retains its full value only if it is potential), calling for a difficult heroic attitude on the part of the assembled groups.[26]

Such is Artaud's view of the kind of thing which is capable of happening when pity and fear are theatrically 'purged'. The urge to be involved and delivered at the same time in the same process is not expended but liberated, set free to work actively within the world. This is the 'other side' of theatre (what Artaud calls "son double"), a world away from 'mere entertainment', yet depending on the same theatrical mechanism – here used in fulfilment of its true potential, dealing with situations that call for violent intervention. Theatre, says Artaud, like plague

> unravels conflicts, liberates powers, releases potential, and if these and the powers are dark, this is not the fault of the plague or theatre, but life.[27]

Looking back on what I have written up to now, since starting out with Thorndike's cat, I am struck with how dull it is, or at least pedestrian, and this is a very great pity. Theatre is never dull. It can be a place of intense, even extreme emotions for the actors and the audience as well as the play's characters themselves. For example, actors are commonly considered to be highly strung. The same could probably be said for some audience members, but not of audiences in general. Actors say that they find having to make an entrance a terrifying experience, and I know myself how very true this is. It is also something which refuses to become easier, however much experience an actor may have. (I have a particularly vivid memory of trying to calm a distinguished Shakespearean actress as she got ready to make her way on-stage, which involved actually walking through the audience to get there. I had only just started my career: she on the other hand, had been acting professionally for at least thirty years. However, this did not stop her clinging onto the frame of the door, incapable of any kind of movement, as she waited for the arrival of the cue which alone possessed the power to galvanise her into life.)

Audiences undergo other kinds of emotionally testing experience: I leave it to the reader to recall times when she or he has felt themselves torn apart by plays which have suddenly become unbearably personal to them. Having drawn us gently in, theatre proceeds to generate in intense power which it exerts over us. Some, like Bertolt Brecht,[28] have complained about the kind of theatre which aims at manipulating the audience by playing on their feelings, overpowering their judgement with "a tidal wave of emotion", so that they leave the theatre with their judgement distorted – or, what is worse, rid of the feelings of responsibility towards their fellow human beings which it is theatre's job to arouse and not simply purge away.

Because of their determination not to take advantage of an audience's emotional gullibility by pretending to be anything other than fiction, stories performed by actors, Brecht's plays have an intense emotional effect. Actors call this kind of theatre 'playing against the scene', which means giving the impression that you yourself are not moved (in case the audience might think that it is you to whom these things are happening and so assume that the character you are playing is real). From the audience's point of view, however, this kind of acting turns out to be extremely moving, as it makes room for the beholder's imagina tion, which too convincing an impersonation on the actor's part, too close an identification with the character, can sometimes prevent. When this happens onlookers are more impressed by an actor's 'realism', his or her ability to 'be' the person, than by the significance of what is actually being said; and this may well get in the way of the message delivered by the play as a whole.

This, of course, is simply another example of the power of aesthetic distance; of the gap calling out to be filled and our own eagerness to be the ones filling it. Brecht was right, of course: those presenting the play bear the final responsibility for the meaning of the event, and we should not be bullied into agreeing with them. On the other hand our responsiveness is our own, as is the imagination we bring with us which is able to excite us so powerfully, stirring in us such depths of emotion, some of it familiar but not all, so that we find ourselves moved by things we never took much notice of before; certainly not *personally* that is. The truth is that these things to do not work if they are forced. An actress well known for her television performances told me: "One thing is essential: never strive."[29] I wish she had warned me earlier, at the beginning of my own career in theatre.

This actress didn't tell me that I should not allow myself to feel. She simply said that good acting did not involve the imposition of feelings on the audience. She said that the same principle held for the actor's approach to her or his part. Read the play and let it come, she said; allow it to come of its own accord:

> Don't go working hard to 'get under your character's skin' as so many acting teachers urge you to do. Don't work on your character, let him or her work on you. When the time is ripe you'll move in all right.

This is aesthetic distance again, the pull of dramatic space, as powerful for television performance as it is for stage ones, because it is the milieu in which imagination works – the opportunity for it to do its work somewhere where it can be shared with others.

The 'space between',[30] whether it separates us from each other or from another part of ourselves, is always potentially explosive. We may use our technical skill to signify it in any number of ways, without being able to tie it down. It is both elusive and available, acting as a permeable barrier between separate existences. In itself it lays down no rules, except that of being without any, which is why it allows things which the ordinary ways of coping with life by containing it have no room for; extreme things which are too fragile or too violent to be spoken, or perhaps even thought about in other circumstances. But whether its effect is to calm us or arouse our passions it is never dull in the way which life outside the play can be. Even plays about boredom, in which the characters complain about the absence of things which would give interest to their lives – like *The Cherry Orchard*[31] or *Waiting for Godot*[32] – manage to sustain an audience's interest because of the expectation that in a play something is bound to happen, because this is what plays are for: they let us in on what is happening between people, and they also do so in a setting in which even other people's frustration manages to hold our attention. Frustration creates space, as we wait longingly for something to happen. Theatre space not only demands to be filled but enables us to fill it; and the longer the wait, the more passionate our response is likely to be.

CHAPTER FOUR

CATS AND BAGS

"This must be a simply enormous wardrobe!" thought Lucy, going still further in and pushing the soft folds of the coats aside to make room for her. Then she noticed that there was something crunching under her feet. "I wonder, is that more mothballs?" she thought, stooping down to feel it with her hand.[33]

It was not mothballs that Lucy was feeling but snow. She had pushed her way into Narnia, the land where, because of the White Witch, it is "Always winter and never Christmas." This was a very special wardrobe she had decided to hide in. On one side it was standing in the old house where she was playing hide-and-seek with her sister and brothers, but on the other it was a gateway to a different place altogether.

The story is C.S. Lewis's *The Lion, the Witch and the Wardrobe*, a seemingly innocuous title, but one which is overflowing with significance for this and all other *Tales of Narnia* because it immediately presents us with the materials from which they are made and the requirements placed upon the reader by the author himself. All three narrative elements – lion, witch and wardrobe – are archetypal, possessing infinitely greater resonance than might at first be supposed: Aslan is a lion and more than a lion; The White Witch more than a cruel and selfish tyrant; the wardrobe more than a wardrobe. It is the wardrobe, of course, which holds the clue to this. The prosaic piece of furniture symbolises its own opposite, opening up quite literally into poetry and possessing the power to take us with it. Aslan and the Witch balance each other as Good and Evil, generation and sterility, and herein lies the drama which provides the plot of the stories; but the role of the wardrobe is to allow there to be a story at all.

The wardrobe stands for disclosure. The story signals itself as a story by surprising us. Surprise is what we both expect and ask for; otherwise we are unwilling to regard what is happening as a story and allow ourselves to entertain it as such and suspend disbelief in it. The surprise need not come at the beginning: we are perfectly willing to wait for gratification because we know that, somewhere along the line something will happen which will surprise us; in order to justify its calling itself a story in the first place.

So close is this identification of story and surprisingness that even when we have heard the story before – even many times before – we are able to recall the original amazement it aroused in us and enjoy it again in imagination. This is because it is not only the presence of something unexpected which holds our attention, but the *kind* of unexpectedness involved. The Narnia stories are full of unforeseen events and startling reversals of fortune, but none is so important as the backless wardrobe which, as the gateway into Narnia, allows everything else to happen. Story is not merely a narrative involving a degree of surprise, it is a surprising narrative, one which is improbable by definition – the world of fiction, generally considered to exist within its own dimension, and as such open to being seen as the opposite of truth. From this point of view it becomes apparent that the identity of Narnia as fiction does not depend on the presence within the story of the Professor's bookcase, but in the fact that we are presented from the outset with something which never claims to be anything else. The surprise is one we have been familiar with all our lives. What is unexpected however is that, while assuring ourselves of our rationality, we continue to be taken in. But then, being taken in turns out to be an archetypal experience.

As such it undergirds our imagination, however determined we may be to control it in accordance with our natural preference for realities which we consider to be dependable, in a practical sense. One such reality is the usefulness of story as a way of teaching well-defined and recognisable ideas about how life should be lived – what might be called the parabolic use of story, where the listener is exhorted, either explicitly or implicitly, to grasp what she or he has heard (or read) in terms of certain abstract principles, the important thing being not the story itself but what it is actually saying to the listener. It follows from this, of course, that the events recounted should not in any way intrude on the message to be communicated.

In other words, it should not be too dramatic, because drama, by calling on an act of imaginative involvement, encourages us to believe that things are really going on, whereas restraint put on our credulousness permits us to keep a clear head about what is fiction and what is not. This is particularly hard to sustain when the story is being acted out in our presence, as happens in the theatre. Brecht called some of his plays 'Parables'; but it is the play itself which seizes our imagination, and the degree of emotion which it arouses in us which we remember, even though we are constantly reminded by the playwright that we should not allow our judgement to be clouded by our natural response to the things which are happening on stage.[34]

These things cannot avoid being dramatic because they are *happening*, not simply being thought or even talked about. This makes them events rather than propositions. This can be a profoundly shocking experience, having the force of fact even when as ideas they seem hypothetical, or even in some cases, highly unlikely. Such experiences are pivotal for theatre. In *Richard III*, for example, there is a scene in which Richard accosts Lady Anne as she follows her husband's body to the grave. He has himself played an important part in this man's death and yet he chooses this moment to pay court to his widow:

Teach not thy lip such scorn, for it was made
For kissing, lady, not for such contempt.
Lo, here I tend thee this sharp-pointed sword.
(He lays his breast open: she offers at it with his sword.)
Nay, do not pause; for I did kill King Henry
But 'twas thy beauty that provoked me.
Nay, now despatch; 'twas I that stabb'd young Edward.
(She again offers at his breast.)
But 'twas thy heavenly face that set me on.
(She lets fall the sword.)[35]

This is dramatic enough on the page, considering the scenario presented to the imagination – the sorrowful woman herself, the brazen effrontery of Richard's invasion of her grief, the abusive assertion of sexuality, the shocking suggestion of offence given to the corpse by this interruption of the rites held by human beings everywhere in the world to be his due, even the rage of the dead man himself at seeing his daughter-in-law dishonoured by the treacherous Richard; all this is profoundly disturbing to contemplate, and likely to stay in the memory of anyone reading the play as the most shockingly outrageous of Richard's villainies, the one which teaches us most about his character.

Nevertheless, to see it being enacted in the theatre is even more unforgettable, because it gives rise to the phenomenon which belongs only to plays presented by live actors to living audiences: 'theatre-shock'. Theatre-shock is the experience of seeing something impossible happening; and this is what is actually taking place here. When Richard bares his breast to Lady Anne – in this way, at this time, under these circumstances – we, the audience find ourselves rendered incapable of knowing how to react. And yet it is happening: we are shocked into acceptance, our disbelief short-circuited by the event, by what is there before us, and it will take us some time to regain our balance – if indeed we ever do whilst the play is going on. The effect is similar to the way in which people involved in traffic accidents describe post-traumatic stress which, they say, is the result of finding yourself unable to do anything at all to deal with a situation from which you have no way of escaping and are rendered panic stricken and immobile . . . [36]

That, of course, is something which happens in life outside the theatre. In plays the condition is rendered less extreme by the circumstances, by being in a place where fact and fiction are held in balance. The balance, however, is a precarious one, and we can still be shocked out of it by things which disturb it from either direction, by being too dramatic or simply not dramatic enough. Richard's behaviour is certainly disturbing, even though, having reached this point in the play we know very well what to expect from him. We are not, however, surprised by Richard's actions, which we could quite easily imagine anyway in the light of our knowledge of him, but by *seeing it happen*; seeing it happen and not being able to stop it!

For all our involvement in what is going on, there is nothing whatever that we can do. We can neither get into the arena nor out of the theatre. So why did we choose to come in the first place? Surely this has happened to us before – the experience of being shocked into believing against our will so that we are left to regret the devastating effect it has had on our own sense of autonomy; surely this is simply the kind of thing we should expect once we start playing this sort of game. After all, it was we ourselves who undertook to suspend our disbelief, so we have no reason to complain if we find theatre taking us at our word and taking us farther than we really wanted to go, and in a direction of its choosing, not ours.

We come because we know that this shocking experience is not all theatre has to offer. In other words, that is not the end of the story we have chosen to become partners in believing in. Soon enough, rather sooner than such things happen in the world outside the theatre, the play reasserts itself as play and balance is restored once more. The shock of whatever has happened to disturb our emotional equilibrium draws attention to the necessity of reasserting it. This is why I referred to 'theatre-shock' as pivotal; by leaping out of the frame plays direct our awareness towards the frame itself, the structure which contains them and is the condition for them existing for us in a way which is able to make the kind of sense from which we are able to benefit. Trauma and theatre go together.[37] This propensity for 'leaping from the page' expressing itself in events which, when transported into the theatre, are both completely impossible and totally convincing, is the form taken by the dramatic archetype itself.

They are also the most striking expression of the cathartic effect of theatre, its ability to give scope to pent up feelings. These *coups de théatre* are associated in the memories and imaginations of theatre goers with feelings of joyful surprise connected with being unexpectedly released from the pressures of deciding what should be done next; just as the play reaches a point of sudden impossibility, and by doing so gives itself room for new possibilities to take root, so we the audience and actors are made aware of our own personal freedom and the existence of a way out for us, too.

This is not something we expected. When, remembering the benefit of having done so in the past, we agreed to trust the play and try to go along with it, we were not counting on being rendered impotent in this way. Gaining our freedom at the end of the journey is no surprise because we have been there before. The way in which we are delivered, however, is always a surprise, as is the quality of the emotion it stirs up when we discover how, amazingly, the lid of the box has been raised.

It is in this amazing confrontation with Lady Anne that we are shown what the Richard III which Shakespeare is in the process of creating for us is really like:

'Twas thy heavenly face that set me on.
(She lets fall the sword.)

In such ways theatre 'lets the cat out of the bag'. Sometimes it is by unexpected things which people say or do, sometimes by what they simply ignore – as in the scene in John Osborne's *Look Back in Anger*, when Alison has burned her arm while doing the ironing:

CLIFF: *(kneeling on the arm of her chair)* Give it here. *(She holds out her arm.)* Yell out if I hurt you. *(He bandages it for her.)*
ALISON: *(staring at her outstretched arm)* Cliff –
CLIFF: Um? *(slight pause)* What is it, lovely?
ALISON: Nothing.
Cliff: I said; what is it?
ALISON: You see – *(hesitates)* I'm pregnant.
CLIFF: *(after a few moments)* I'll need some scissors.
ALISON: They're over there.[38]

In those 'few moments' the frustrated love which Cliff bears for both Alison and her husband Jimmy flashes out to illuminate him as a person, and consequently the crucial role he plays in the story. In this short exchange, he becomes alive; and he does this, not by what he says, but by the way he hesitates. The way he refrains from saying anything at all.

These are unexpected reactions. They are the stock-in-trade of drama and its very essence. These are two very different kinds of play, one a sixteenth century poetic melodrama, the other a piece of social realism from the mid-twentieth century. Both, however, are full of surprises. In theatre, however, even boredom can be surprising, or rather it can contribute to the expectation of the unexpected which we experience at the prospect of drama. In the broadest sense a play like *Three Sisters* is hardly dramatic at all because nothing very much seems to be happening in it, so that it might easily be dismissed as a failure from the dramatic point of view. In fact, of course, the opposite is the case. In plays like this – and they are really quite common – the need to be surprised is palpably starved and its gratification postponed to the point at which things which would otherwise have seemed trivial now have the power to startle us, like the sudden appearance of 'four or five' leaves on the tree between the acts of *Waiting for Godot*.[39]

In *Godot* it is something which the scenery does rather than the characters, but this is a play in which the setting speaks almost as clearly, almost as much as a character, as the people living in it. Certainly the *mise en scène* plays a part in the action of any play at all, particularly if it tries not to do so ; even so it is what the people are doing which makes it a play in the first place; and particularly the surprising things which they do or do not do. Sometimes these are for the benefit of the other people in the play itself – as with Richard and Anne – and sometimes for that of the audience, as in the scene in the second part of *Henry IV* when Prince Henry, sitting at the bedside of his sleeping father, picks up the dying king's crown and tries it on for size:

Lo, here it sits. *(Putting it on his head)*[40]

This is the most revealing evidence of all as to what a character is like, what kind of person she or he really is. This is more convincing than what other characters say, because they always say it from a particular point of view – their own – and we would rather wait to make up our own minds, believing ourselves to be less biased; and the same holds for characters who take it upon themselves to speak directly to us. They too are open to the possibility of special pleading. What characters actually *do* is different.

What they are seen to do. What, in fact, we witness their doing. At these times, in these places, we are liberated from the necessity to suspend disbelief by events which cut across anything we must do in order to be in the right frame of mind to take part in the play. Up to now we have been concentrating on the creative results of our participation in other people's inventiveness; now we are seized by immediacy, by people who say and do things which leap aesthetic distance and hit us between the eyes with their actuality.

When this happens characters become people, and we encounter them as themselves. The awareness of performance, of a situation in which actors are impersonating fictional persons, figments of their own and the playwright's imagination, is immediately forgotten, as if this were the only reality and our involvement with these people were a matter of personal importance or even concern. Suddenly, their business has become ours, too; and so the play comes to life, not only as metaphor but as the encounter of persons.

Theatre shocks us into belief, so that believing, we may respond as we would like to do in our own lives outside the theatre, by sharing others' emotions and apportioning them a stake in our own. Protected by the fiction of the drama we feel at liberty to think and feel things here which we would be frightened to do outside because, here in the theatre, the world of the play, these things may be given safe expression. Or so we think. Somehow the impact of theatrical presentation, its *thisness* and *hereness* lays hold of our awareness in a way we had forgotten that it could do. In such moments disbelief is short-circuited not by ideas but people – real live people, able to seize us by the throat or have us rolling in the aisles – or whatever well-tried metaphor comes to hand for describing the indescribable.

Theatre, then, is a shocking business, not only because some of the stories it delivers are deliberately intended to have this effect on us, but because arresting our attention in ways which hook us into immediate awareness is its stock-in-trade. An actor in a Goldoni farce jumps off the stage in the midst of the duel, which is surprising. When, by mistake, he appears to have stabbed one of the audience, the effect upon the rest of us is electric.[41] or, to take a better known example, we are able to share Hamlet's distress at his mother's remarriage, although we may perhaps be a little disconcerted by the extreme nature of his reaction. This obviously is genuine mental anguish, and we feel something of it ourselves:

> O! that this too too solid flesh would melt
> Thaw and resolve itself into a dew;
> Or that the Everlasting had not fix'd
> His canon 'gainst self-slaughter!
> O God! O God![42]

But when, later in the play, he finds himself an unseen spectator at Ophelia's interment and vaults into her grave:

> this is I
> Hamlet the Dane. (*Leaps into the grave.*)[43]

we make personal contact with *him*.

The surprises of theatre unlock the reality of its characters for us. We need, however, to go deeper if we want to know how theatre works. It is not enough to be made aware of the characters as real people. We need to know what it is that makes them exist at all, what allows them to be people for us, and this involves our knowing more about the context of the disclosure. For our picture to have any background, we need to know the whole story.

CHAPTER FIVE

JOURNEYING

Everyman, stand still! Whither art thou going
Thus gaily? Hast thou thy maker forgot?[44]

This is Death, who has come to Everyman, called here in this
medieval morality play to answer on behalf of all of us for the
lives we lead here on earth. Because our life is time-bound we
cannot remain in one condition, one place that is, for ever; and,
for Everyman the time has come to move on: "On thee thou must
take a long journey . . . " In fact, says Death, this will be his final
journey, one which will end in the need for a final reckoning
made before the throne of God. Along with the rest of us he has
been God's steward, and now the time approaches for him to
render his account:

What, weenest thou thy life is given thee
And thy worldly goods also?.[45]

The main action of the play stretches onwards from here until
the hero arrives at the place where his tomb is and he must say
goodbye to the companions who have supported him until now
– by no means the ones to whom he originally looked for to assist
him on his final journey – and take the final steps entirely alone.
Thus the purpose of the play is specifically didactic. As
'Knowledge', who had been with him almost to the end, solemnly
informs us:

Now hath he suffered that we shall all endure.

All the same, this is very different from a religious treatise or
even a sermon. *Everyman* is a piece of authentic theatre delivering its message as plays do, by means of a sequence of events

which progresses from problem to solution by way of dramatic reversals of expectations. Here the crux of the action lies in the hero's catastrophic discovery that 'Good Deeds', on whom he has relied for his ultimate salvation, is already, through neglect on his part, much too week to offer him any real help; without this he would never have turned back, learning trust for God's mercy rather than his own efforts. The ideas may be abstract but the impact is powerful. We know what these characters will do and say simply by hearing their names. Their presence as people surprises us so that we find ourselves having to go a little deeper. Theatre speaks more convincingly about destiny than moral lectures can, since plays allow their characters to speak to others on behalf of themselves.

All plays are not the record of a life-career to the same extent as *Everyman*. Plays, however, do normally concentrate on the significance of the passing of time in the lives of the people portrayed, using their own relationship with time, which is that of a real event, having a beginning, a middle and an end, as a way of directing the audience's attention to the fact that these people's lives had shape and purpose; and that such things are characteristic of human lives, including the audience's own. This is the truth of theatre, says the play, the reason why it exists; and what, at this particular point in your lives, you find yourselves actually engaged in sharing with your fellows, is its archetypal expression.

However it does not say it very loudly in case it puts us off. Audiences object to being subjected to sermons – perhaps they always did, even in *Everyman's* time – which may be the reason for trying to convince the onlookers that they were really concerned with abstract categories, not living characters. Drama's approach is not so obvious, even in the setting up of role models. We are much more likely to be impressed by the tale of Pericles,[46] so that we admire his integrity and pay homage to the faithfulness of his searching than we ever could be by Everyman's all-too-human narrative, however moving its final scenes turn out to be.

Pericles, of course, is not a religious play in the *Everyman* sense. The closest we might get to claiming it is would be by recognising that it holds within itself an awareness of human destiny which some would see as implicitly religious, or at least deeply spiritual. There are religious people in it – not as allegories but as themselves: Thaissa, the beloved wife whom Pericles had thought to have died tragically in giving birth to his daughter Marina, returns to his side having become High Priestess of Diana's Temple, but this is intended to come as a surprise rather than as the play's main point, the message which it sets out to communicate. This it finally succeeds in bringing home, along with the two women he loves best:

> ... no more, you Gods! Your present kindness
> Makes my past miseries sport.[47]

Theatre reminds us vividly of something we must remember in order to survive: that without failure success is meaningless, and that whatever we have achieved, we will have no ways of enjoying it unless we have encountered setbacks along the way and suffered accordingly. This obvious truth tends to be something which we prefer to ignore. Theatre, however, is a way of underlining it; its purpose is the recognition of shape within our lives. From this point of view the two plays we have been considering, *Everyman* and *Pericles*, stand for a whole host of others insofar that all plays aimed at portraying human inter-reality may be described as examples of the way that human beings tell stories to and about one another.

"Are you sitting comfortably?" says the storyteller: "then I'll begin." The pause before she or he does so, like the empty space in a theatre, summons our awareness and we wait expectantly to be told where to shift our sights so that we may make our way into the imaginary world prepared for us. First we must be briefed so that we can recognise persons, places and times when we encounter them:

> Once upon a time in a country far away, there lived a young man.
> The young man was a prince. He lived with the King and Queen
> in a palace at the foot of a mountain ...

This information is of the greatest importance. If it is omitted the usefulness of the narrative as a story will be seriously impaired as its relevance for things already understood, which corresponds to its ability to refer to situations, places and people in real life, will be lost. It may have abstract value as a pattern of ideas but if we are to learn anything about what it is like to be alive, then we need to know the facts – we can be kept guessing by the technique of 'delayed exposition' so popular with directors of television drama, but this itself is only in order to increase our eagerness to get things properly under way.

This sort of background information is, of course, vital for all further developments. Even if storytelling is a joint effort, as often happens within therapeutic settings where an individual co-operates with a group of others to create a shared story, each of them adding a stage in a tale that is unfolding round the circle, it is essential to establish the 'where, who and what' of the point of origin. In improvised drama these markers must be clearer than ever, because the story which follows has as yet neither extension nor actual existence, so the temptation to whet the listeners' appetites with an exciting foretaste of adventures yet to come doesn't arise. Instead, those taking part must undertake to start the story in an explicit way by 'inventing themselves' – "I am Donald, a Scottish historian, my wife has just had a baby. Will I be able to cope?"' "Mrs Muriel Griffiths, I run a boarding house. I have trouble with my best friend who keeps pressing me to go into business with her."; "I'm either a burglar or a milkman, according to the time of day."

Making plays up in situ like this draws attention to the fact that identity comes first in storytelling of any kind. We need to know whom it is we are supposed to be listening to. Some roles are so familiar that we find we can take those who inhabit them on trust – roles like storyteller, presenter, actor – but who are these people in the drama? Why should we even consider staying to hear their story if we don't know who they are?

The same is true of the ends of stories which, if anything, are more important than their beginnings. There is always a possibility that even if we fail to register a character's identity at the beginning we will have been able to gain a firmer grasp on who they are by the end in the course of discovering how they belong within the total action. In the light of this cumulative disclosure of what the story is really about, we discover that in fact we failed to know who the characters in it really were until we have accompanied them on their journey and arrived with them in the new state of affairs. This, we say, is the story's meaning; we didn't really know what was happening until now, until the process of making it happen was complete. We didn't know where it was all going; certainly, we say to the characters, we didn't know *you* . . .

Knowledge of who people are comes from sharing experiences with them. In the story-metaphor it arises from being fellow-travellers on a journey. Whatever form this may take in the story its significance is spiritual and consequently trans-temporal. It is the kind of journey which is only really identifiable as such when it has reached its destination and we become aware that 'end' also means purpose achieved. As we saw in the first chapter, the end of the story is the point of delivery for its message. Not, however, for what it actually means: endings, like beginnings, clear a space round themselves, to be used this time for reflection rather than imagination, as we look back on where the story has taken us and apply it to ourselves.

Which brings us to the main action, the events happening in the story which make it worth telling. Here the attention focused at the beginning is given its main task, that of coping with something for which it is unprepared. The central part of the story describes an unexpected crisis in which the person or people concerned are faced with what they perceive as an insurmountable problem; they know immediately – and we know with them – that nothing can be done. This presence of the unimaginable unmanageable cuts across the story, bringing it to a standstill, stopping it dead in its tracks. At this midpoint in its career no story exists, only an aborted attempt at telling one.

Or so the characters think. In fact, of course, this, and their reaction to it, *is* the story. Somehow or other those involved do survive. They live to tell the tale. The story's interest depends largely on how they manage to do this, but its emotional impact belongs to the fact of their doing it at all. The circumstances of their deliverance make it plain that this was far from being something which they brought off on their own, by their own skill and hard work; quite the opposite, in fact. So much is unforgettably clear to the people who are most closely concerned, who number themselves among those

Led on by heaven and crowned with joy at last.[4]

This central movement within the story is the element in its construction which gives it its special power to move us. In a literal sense it is what the story is *about*, as the narrative is arranged on either side of it, with a departure and a homecoming separated by its location at the centre as the point of balance. Disaster and deliverance occurring together in the same place provide the story's dynamism, expressing something which transcends ordinary logical ways of thinking, consisting as it does in the simultaneous presence of opposites. There are many metaphors for this: the fulcrum on which the story turns,; the anvil for it to be beaten into shape; the heart beating its blood; the mind giving it form and meaning; the lungs pumping the air by which it lives and breathes, the epi-centre.[48]

Perhaps the distinctive thing about stories and the plays which embody them is the location of their meaning not at the beginning or end, but in the middle. Hence understanding them means getting involved in them. In practical terms it depends on our willingness to set out upon the journey of discovery signified by the form which they take. This is the form of an experience that is interrupted and resumed, the original purpose having been transformed by the interruption into something – somewhere – else. In effect, the story is *healed*, and in the healing of stories we see the healing of lives.

The religious significance of this is immediately apparent. Throughout the world, in one way or another, story articulates mankind's yearning for ultimate wholeness. Sometimes story and religious faith are closely identified, to the extent that the latter finds expression only in story form, whether as historical account or divinely inspired tradition. Sometimes the religious significance is less explicit, and peace of mind, a less specific hopefulness, is the reward for our co-journeying. Perhaps the most valuable thing of all is the simple discovery of the power of imagination to mediate truthful experience, our awareness of what we perceive as our own reality.

Unless we ourselves are artists we are not used to rating imagination as highly as this. As suggested in Chapter One, we tend to regard it as useful for playing games of one kind or another, but not for the serious business of living; certainly not for situations calling for honesty and the preservation of integrity. We use it for these purposes because we are unable to think about ourselves without it; we even need it in order to criticise ourselves for using it. We object to the fact that we are unable to tie it down, even though we know our world is perpetually moving under us so that the last things we need in order to manage being alive in it are static categories, measurable phenomena, to distract us from our real business, our ongoing need to find out which way our life is going so that we can keep up with it.

Story reminds us that we are creatures on the move. This is its true identity, its main purpose. We associate it with childhood, the time when we set out learning how to learn, and this is why we tend to regard it as less important once we have grown up. Perhaps we think of it as a stage in developing the ability to cope with real people and things, something we have a definite obligation to 'grow out of'. We are often told this, so we shouldn't be surprised if we end up believing it, but we never grow out of our dependence on storytelling and story acting, because we never grow out of ourselves.

Donald Winnicott[49] invented the term 'transitional object' to describe the part played by imagination in the development of our ability to form personal relationships. It describes an object of some kind – a doll, a rag, a teddy bear, a wooden spoon – which the child imagines to be alive and consequently able to be treated as a person; the only difference being that this thing/person is able to survive situations and events which cause trouble in relationships with the real people whom the child comes up against. (To put it bluntly, you can bash a teddy against the wardrobe and it doesn't *really* die . . .)

The point about the transitional objects is that they are engaged in going somewhere, carrying on their journey their owner/friends/lovers. The movement is in two opposite directions, because the play object is used to hide from the life of other people as well as grow more involved in it. Similarly the child herself or himself is in two minds as to whether Teddy is alive. Teddy is in both places at once; he is a symbol of the union of baby and mother at the time these are becoming separate in the baby's mind.[50] The parents of small children know intuitively not to question this way of looking at the world, recognising it as the child's present reality. For the time being they do what people do when they watch a play and "suspend their disbelief".

For the time being. The principle holds for longer, however. In fact it remains true for the rest of our lives, that things we invest with reality are real for us and for as many as we can persuade to share our experience with; the complete experience that is, including the part played in it by the imagination. Winnicott was in no doubt that the ability to think beyond whatever is usually regarded as reasonable was the foundation of "that cultural aspect of human life including art, philosophy and religion".[51] Whenever we invest our stories with meaning and allow the truth which sleeps within them to awaken and play its part in our lives we are vindicating story and bestowing credibility on the act of imagining reality.

Scientists assure us that science depends on art, if only because theorising has to be an exercise of imagination. We test our facts by our willingness to invest them in fiction. In this way we expect to draw a dividend of practical – *i.e.* usable – knowledge. Throughout our lives we repeat the childhood strategy of using imagination to 'try life out for size'. We turn playfulness into objectivity by standing back from ourselves so as to be in a position to choose from a range of alternative scenarios the one most likely to achieve the result we are aiming for. The scenarios are fictional. They are the stories we tell ourselves about things which might or could or probably will happen in our lives, each possibility having its own storyline. The results, however, have to be factual, concerned with the realities involved in living together in a world which remains resistant to the stories we tell about it, although we ourselves may be convinced by them. Stories which become publicly convincing, as Winnicott points out, attain the status of truths widely shared. The principle remains the same: we move away from our established reality in order to draw it after us. The motive power is imagination. We are surrounded by story.

CHAPTER SIX

TRUSTING

O, this feeds my soul.[52]

Faustus is in Hell. He is watching a pageant specially mounted for him by Mephistopheles (and of course, for us too by Christopher Marlowe). Even in Hell he is delighted by what he sees, for here as everywhere, the play beckons, as the theatre and its players work together to involve us, playing hard upon our imagination to draw us into their world. It is the story which intrigues, the subject matter of people, places and human intentions, reminding us of ourselves and the things we get up to in being ourselves; but it is also *how* it does it, for plays treat stories in a particular way. Stories draw attention to their significance by way of arranging the events they are dealing with – their subject matter – in a particular way which we refer to as 'dramatic' because it derives from the theatrical presentation of plays. If, when it becomes a story, something happens to a plain record of events to bring out its particular relevance to ourselves, then the same kind of thing happens to stories which become the material for acted drama, the embodiment of personal experience which is theatre.

Plays actively invite us in, using living people to do so. In theatre person encounters person in exploring the personal; or in Faustus's case, a demonic impersonation of it. The vision of the splendours of Mephistopheles's kingdom is potent enough to convince Faustus because he is seized by the story to be lived out, he himself being its triumphant hero. The characters in the spectacle enacted before him ask him to share it with them, as do the imaginary personages in any play, saying "Do you see? What do you think and feel about this?" If they don't talk to us in so many words (and sometimes they do) they do in the things they say to one another and in the way they behave.

The story of the play has a shape which articulates its meaning, delivering a meta-message[53] on the subject of what the play is about. In some way or other it symbolises the triumph of life, the purpose of purpose. This is compulsory, remaining the case whether the treatment is serious or light-hearted; however expressed, the story is one of creative reversal. Even plays in which nothing seems to happen, such as Samuel Beckett's *Waiting for Godot*[54] represent the triumph of the human spirit as deferred hope is a whole universe away from actual despair: "We'll hang ourselves tomorrow," Gogo says, placing his emphasis firmly on the last word.

Story presents an image of meaning, the outline of an achievable purpose. However, signalling its presence is only part of what stories do; their real business is to bring it to life. Stories are inhabited ideas. It is the characters who live in them who make contact with us, as everybody who can tell the difference between a story and an instruction manual is very well aware. Nowhere is this more obvious than in the theatre, as the story lets us in on not only what is happening but to whom – to these people here and our part in them. Action depends on setting and setting on story. Here the action is embodied; alive on both sides of the central, unifying space, and whatever happens here, happens *now*. Characters lend their lives to what has been plotted beforehand to give it immediacy and make it a place for living, not simply thinking, in.

It is what happens that brings the characters and ourselves to life. It is what they do and say *because* of the unfolding narrative, that allows us to know them. As Aristotle insisted, "the plot is the soul of the drama."[55] As its soul, it gives life to the entire dramatic structure, embracing all who take part in it by suspending their disbelief to the point of willingness to become part of the world it creates, for the time it takes to do so.

If drama creates space, then plot is responsible for controlling time. The duration of a play is as long as it takes to unfold the plot. The entire plot, not just a part of it. Like the cat, to get the message so that we really know it, have authentically lived it, we must learn to do it in sequence. We do this under the authority of our imagination, whereas the cat actually learns the box. In this case 'learning in sequence' means doing so in terms of the plot, by following the story through. Certainly, unlike cats we can stand back and draw conclusions: but not yet. Not until the curtain has fallen . . .

The cat enjoys his puzzle box. Now it is his, not Thorndike's, and he keeps coming back to play with it. (I'm using my imagination, of course!) As he goes through the process of getting free again he resists others' attempts to help him by pointing to the solution before he himself is ready to discover it. He is busy and doesn't wish to be bothered with anything else, any more than we want to have to get up and leave the theatre before the last act, particularly as plays generate more suspense half way through than at any other stage of the plot. We demand the right to see things through, rather than simply abandoning ship when the going gets tough, thus leaving our imaginary comrades and fellow travellers to drown.

Put like this it looks absurd. After all, we are talking about suspending our disbelief, not abandoning it altogether; and cats may be observed to get bored rather easily, particularly if the danger arises of having to miss the next meal. All the same, the argument manages to bear weight: the cat learns the box, being in it in order to do so, and we absorb the play, going along with the plot so we can say we have really seen it and not just read the review. We get inside the play by our own ability to imagine what someone is experiencing when the particular events dictated by the plot are taking place. The efforts we make to keep reminding ourselves that the world of the play is not ours are proof that, emotionally at least, this is our world – it is because it could be. Emotionally we are in the play, trying to keep our heads above the water, hampered in doing so by the persistence of imagination, its power not to deny thought, but to contain it; for a period of time to encompass it.

The plot is our time-keeper, authorised to shut us in and let us out again. It has power over us, as it does over the personages within the play, having been put together without our knowledge; certainly without consulting us. Neither we nor they have any real idea where it will take us next. Even in extemporised drama no-one knows this apart from the next person who speaks, whoever that may be. We can guess, of course. As personages within the drama we can draw conclusions and make plans, but if the plot dictates otherwise they are bound to fall by the wayside: the plot is in charge whatever happens. We have put ourselves in its hands, so that in the long run we have to make our arrangements accordingly, adjusting our stage lives in conformity to an outcome that has already been decided – or one which can be imposed arbitrarily at any stage in the drama.

In other words, whether we are participating as actors or audience, we are in the hands of whoever it was that put together this particular plot. This is true about any kind of story, of course, whether it be intended to be read silently or aloud to other people, or acted before an audience. If we are going to use our imagination in such a way we must provide it with material to work on, a *mise en scène* for us to bring to life and share with one another. Furthermore this sketched-in background must always be definite enough to provide the setting for realistically drawn characters. A certain amount of plotting is necessary in order to bring the characters alive enough to be impersonated by the actors and, consequently, identified with by an audience.

How much of this theatrical impact is due to plot and how much to the actors? Almost any actor will tell you that it is mainly the plot which brings characters alive: "I'm only as good as my material; we all are." The appeal of theatre to those who dedicate themselves to it rests largely on this question, which again turns out to be a matter of balance: the actor sets out to be as real and yet as transparent as possible; to register but not impose. After all, the actors themselves know where the play is going and what will happen to the character they are playing. The character, however, does not. Actors build their characters on the information supplied by playwrights, balancing what they themselves have to contribute as people who possess their own personal histories with what this character requires in order to be real to the audience within the terms of a specific sequence of events, settings and personalities with which they are currently being presented. In other words, in terms of the plot.

The relationship between plot and character is a source of immense fascination for makers of plays. After all they construct the play, but their characters have to live in it. We are concerned here not with the actors who are carrying out the playwright's instructions as to what will happen in the play, but with the people portrayed within it, whose destiny is decided by the action and who, speaking for themselves, may very well object to the fate assigned to them by the author, wishing that events might turn out in a way which is more in accordance with their own view of the situation they are involved in – and, of course of themselves in particular!

In Pirandello's[56] masterpiece *Six Characters in Search of an Author* the play's characters take over the plot to prevent the audience from being misled by the play about them which is about to be performed by actors hired for the purpose – that is the scenario so painstakingly created for them by the playwright, disposer-in-chief of everything which can possibly happen in a play. On this occasion in this particular production the characters beg to differ:

> THE FATHER: (*to Producer*) I only wish to show you that one is born
> into life in so many forms . . . As a tree or as a stone; in water
> or as a butterfly . . . Or as a woman. And that one can be born
> a character.
> PRODUCER: (*ironically feigning amazement*) And you, together with
> these other people were born a character?
> THE FATHER: Exactly. And alive, as you see . . . [57]

But in fact the Producer's irony is entirely justified, because whether the characters demand the right to put the case in their own ways or not, the authority of the plot abides, merely shifting its ground in order to take account of the unexpected developments. It is a favourite ploy in drama to interrupt the story by introducing elements intended to damage the credibility of the imaginary world which has been created, as the effect is to increase our commitment rather than destroying it, as a broken bone knits together stronger than it was before. Similarly, actors plant a colleague in the audience with instructions to drag everyone's attention away from the play by calling for a doctor or faking a seizure of some kind, so that their eagerness to get back to re-enter the stage-world will now be all the more intense for having been unexpectedly hoaxed in the stalls.

To test the power of the plot by finding ways of loosening its grip strengthens its ability to shape imagination so it can provide truth with a form to be recognised and remembered. Here again, as with other manifestations of the artistic principle, to interrupt a process has the effect of making its expression stronger rather than weaker. In this case it is as if the limits set by the art form, the defining characteristic of the genre, have an invigorating effect on the material constrained by it, so that the stone, paint, musical or verbal phrase or, in this case, stage-character, like the Greek god who sprang to life as a direct result of being thrown to the ground, gains by being held in check. An artist told me, "When you're painting or doing anything like that, you always need something to kick against." In plays like *Six Characters*, the effort to break out of the play's framework gives immense vigour to the fiction; but its strength lies in its failure to do so. This is the triumph of art rather than its abandonment in favour of 'realism'.

The answer to the question about the relative importance of plot and performance turns out to be that the play refuses to answer it, the whole point of theatre being to disarm this kind of destructive analysis, and to do so by leaving itself defenceless in the face of reductionism. Or at least pretending to do this; because it is the apparent naivety of its suggestion that something which is obviously 'made up' may really be used as authentic material for making sense of life which persuades us to take a holiday from the pressure to do this from another direction. Theatre promises to take us somewhere where life has been arranged in order to tell a story which we can grasp firmly enough to apply to the world with which we ourselves are familiar, not just as an idea, but as an experience.

The purpose of the plot is to provide this experience of shape; to clear a space in life for us to experience the balance in events which we long for but which continues to elude us. From this point of view, the plot is the play, arousing imaginative participation from actors and audience and creating characters whose humanity is brought home by the situations it has plotted for them.

Just as story is fundamental to what we usually call our 'ordinary' life (at the same time pointing out to anybody willing to listen, that we don't mean *their* life should be described in such terms), so plot is not to be separated from the special circumstances of theatre. Neither story nor plot, the name we give it when we wish to draw attention to its nature as contrivance, turn out to be reducible to their constituent parts; instead they pass through stages, all of which must be completed in order to achieve their final significance which turns out to be cumulative in its effect – what Gestalt psychologists might identify as 'linear closure.'[58] In this case, however, the event in its extended development consists of individuals in relationship brought to life as audience members and stage characters by the need to make sense of things forced on them by the strict demands of the story.

This is the complicated situation which is brought into being by the disarmingly simple agreement to fall in with the storyteller's suggestion that we should treat what she or he is presenting before us 'as if' it were common fact rather than a harmless piece of fiction; after all, it *is* fiction, even though the demand it manages to make on our emotional life may turn out to be too disturbing, and the impact it has on our personal worldview too radical to be considered entirely harmless. We can still choose whether or not we want to listen; or having decided to do so, if we intend to take any notice of what we hear.

What we cannot do, though, is pick and choose, paying attention to the parts we like and turning a blind eye to those we don't. For one thing, selective involvement is a contradiction in terms, as imagination resists this degree of control, and once we have turned deliberately away we may find it hard to turn back. For another thing, to separate the various stages in the story is to prevent it becoming one at all. This is because to concentrate on a part is to make nonsense of the whole; not merely to distort the message but to prevent anyone ever making sense of it. To arrive at the truth of story we have to follow its plot right through to its ending, for it is in the completion of the story that its truth is articulated for us. We cannot really expect to see the point until we have – at length – found out the plot.

CHAPTER SEVEN

DRAMATISING

"So what did you do?"

"I jumped right in, didn't I?" (Conversation overheard in a pub)

The last two chapters have concentrated on theatrical experience: we have been looking at how plays are presented in spaces prepared for the purpose, where actors and audience are brought face to face and the separation between them allows those playing parts, and the imaginary characters being played by them, to reach across to and be reached to by the people in the audience, something which is much easier to do than to describe. This is intentional, however, because other ways of doing drama are less explicit than this, which makes their ways of working less obvious and their ability to affect their audience appear more surprising.

Because they do not actually bring us into the living presence of the drama which is being performed, cinema, television and radio put more strain on our sense of between-ness, of being drawn into contact with a world which is separate from ours. This means it is that much easier to turn down the invitation to take part, one which is implicit in drama itself. It also means that once we accept it we are more firmly hooked than ever. The danger is, of course, that we allow ourselves to be tricked into believing something which we know, and can demonstrate, to be out of touch with reality – something much easier to do out-side theatres than in them; the rewards, however, are proportionally greater in terms of the imaginative investment required and the more profound involvement in the action of the drama which can be the result. On the other hand, attending the performance does not always improve the experience of drama. As we all know it is better to be gripped by reading a play than bored by bad acting!

The imagination's ability to leap hurdles denied to literal ways of construing life is the driving force of drama in all its manifestations. Differences among the various media called upon to make dramatic use of its power to draw us out of our everyday worlds turn out to be less important than the intentions which underlie its various uses. First of all, is the aim manipulation or collusion? If the first, are we being disarmed for our own benefit or someone else's? It is comparatively easy to find striking examples of 'public welfare' deception in the social psychological experiments of the 1940s and 50s. If the aim is to involve us in a game which we are meant to recognise as such, or at least to do so to begin with, then this needs to be signalled clearly so that we can join in wholeheartedly, in full awareness of what it is we're doing.

These are obviously extremely important considerations, bringing us back to the ways in which we are able to use drama in the informal, unofficial, often unadmitted, way we use it in our everyday contacts with other people when we find ourselves 'putting on an act' for them. This is something which people are unusually unwilling to do because it sounds like a shameful attempt to deceive. It need not be anything of the sort, of course, as dramatisation is used just as easily for the purpose of sharing what something or other felt like when it happened as for inventing things that never happened at all. Even in everyday life, outside the theatre, drama is as capable of establishing, or even creating, truth as it is of distorting it.[59]

Drama specialises in the area of human understanding where the literal and the imaginary overlap. They do so on purpose, in order to open up a way of knowing which is not available to either approach while being of inestimable value as a way of sustaining a balance between them. The language of drama is always ambiguous, urging us at one and the same time to accept and deny its reality – we are to use it as if it were real while staying aware that it is not. If we can succeed in doing this, things which are real will somehow increase in value for us. It is self-conscious in doing this in a way that our use of drama in ordinary human communication often tries not to be; hence the association of drama with things which are obviously contrived, either 'stagey' or intended to imitate life so closely that we will be hoodwinked into never telling the difference . . .

Drama in all its forms stands for this ambiguity which characterises our immediate perception of life at the same time as pointing beyond it. In theatres, the space and the story-in-the-space present an image of journey and arrival, search and discovery, isolation and encounter, which belongs to playmaking itself, imagination at its most primitive yet capable of the very greatest sophistication and profundity. Part of our awareness, the hardworking urge to control life by exerting pressure on it, achieving mastery of the way happiness works by our efforts to expose and tabulate its constituent parts, finds refreshment here, because this space is full of life but empty of any personal sense of urgency. It is a space designed for both involvement and release, a time when we discover that we have left our watches at home and are grateful for our own forgetfulness.

Obviously then, there is something extraordinary about theatre which justifies its being regarded as an expression of culture rather than an ordinary psychological function, one of the ways in which we are bound to perceive the world we live in. Theatre-going is a social occasion, regarded as a special event rather than part of the daily routine. The same could be said about the cinema, or the evenings when we take particular care to stay at home so that we can watch television or listen to the radio. This kind of drama typifies one end of the drama spectrum, what might be described as the public one as distinct from the private theatre described by Erving Goffman,[60] which we use to make our conversation more vivid. There is, however, an even more public use of theatre, one which dispenses with theatre buildings altogether and moves out into the streets and squares to be in a better position for involving those going about their ordinary business of living. This, of course, is carnival.

Mikhail Bakhtin,[61] the Russian cultural philosopher and art critic saw carnival as presenting the most dramatic scenario of all, the confrontation of life and death as acted out in knockabout ways by a special kind of social functionary whose job is to remind us of our human vulnerability and the absurdity of all pretension; in other words, the clown. Clowns stand for "the carnivalesque aesthetic according to which every dogma and ideology is necessarily relativised and shown to be impermanent."[62] In clowning and carnival symbolism is unclouded by any kind of realism. There is no danger of the characters being mistaken for the people representing them, for clowns are not meant to be literal but allegorical, and those wearing clown make-up set out to disguise their humanity in a way that people acting in plays never intend. The reversal, however temporary and superficial, of ordinary inter-personal reality is aimed at release from the pressures associated with that reality, and of assumptions brought about by regarding the form it currently takes as the only possible one.

In this kind of theatre, the theatre of clowns and cavalcades, huge public festivities, the social scene itself is the stage, just as in the days of jesters it was the Court. Even here, though the dramatic dynamic re-asserts itself and the attempt to disguise the actor's humanity, to say to the spectators, "I am only an idea, not a person," fails to convince. In fact it has precisely the opposite effect, as the difference between the disguise and the person wearing it simply arouses our sympathy. In fact it does this with the greatest dramatic effect, as anyone who has been present at a performance of Leoncavallo's *Pagliacci* will bear witness.[63] Drama does not cease to be drama merely by altering the scale and simplifying the characters. Even under conditions in which disbelieving is compulsory, recognisable emotions arouse imaginative involvement.

At the other end of the scale, however, we have dramas in which it is unacceptable to show any signs of not believing the story being presented and, consequently, the good faith of whoever is presenting it. In theatre we are shown what others are thinking and feeling, in circumstances aimed at releasing responsive emotions and ideas in ourselves. In what we usually call real life, this is no easy process because of the wariness we have in the presence of anyone about whom we feel insufficiently confident to 'let down our guard'. Tom Scheff[64] the American sociologist, describes a completely natural tendency for us to 'kid one another along' as a way of gaining time before actually committing ourselves with regard to what it may be that we want to say. We do this, he says, because we are ashamed of what we see as our own vulnerability and are embarrassed by this.

This kind of shame/embarrassment is something which we recognise, once it has been pointed out, in other people, precisely because we are aware of it in ourselves. All the same, in most circumstances we are loath to admit it. Plays, however, are one place where we can feel protected enough to recognise this shame-making fact about ourselves; which is why so many plays, films and television shows are basically about embarrassment. Scheff draws attention to the effect this vulnerability-neurosis has upon our willingness to acknowledge the need we have to accept and be accepted by others – a consciousness caught between contradictory terrors, engulfment and alienation. It is an 'us and them' attitude which affects the behaviour of nations, social classes, religious groups and local communities as well as their individual members. Its impetus is to be found at the most personal level, in the interaction of individuals and their unwillingness to throw themselves on each other's mercy by risking what they fear others may think of them.

As Bakhtin[65] points out, simply by talking honestly to somebody else we put ourselves in their hands for acceptance or rejection; we may think it is our ideas and opinions which are in danger of rebuttal, overlooking how much these things are part of ourselves, to what extent they are pledges of our own identity. In the action of talking to another we either receive or are denied validation of the fact that we are who we think we are, just as they do in talking to us; and this, Bakhtin says, is the irrefutable evidence that we belong together. Nature separates us, allowing us to think of ourselves as if we were self-sufficient, but only fear actually divides us from one another.

Sociology, says Scheff,[66] should recognise the importance of "the emotional/relational level" and stop ignoring the dynamic role played by disguised and ignored feelings in the decisions we make and the entrenched attitudes of mind which they sometimes reveal. We are theoretically aware of the danger of suppressed and denied feelings just as in our daily lives we experience their results at first hand, to our cost, in so many of our relationships; and drama provides a valuable release from the pressure they exert on us. Scheff in particular is very much aware of the sociological benefits of catharsis.

There is more to dramatic catharsis than the power of theatres, whether architectural or imaginary, to arouse feelings at second hand which need to be recognised nearer home. Plays operate explicitly as well as implicitly, presenting us with fictionalised accounts of people and events which act as vivid illustrations of the results of hiding or distorting our emotions in order to deceive ourselves, and consequently others with whom we are in relationship. Drama creates what it describes. Just as we suffer through our involvement with others' pain, we are ourselves unmasked as we witness the removal of other people's disguises and the consequent collapse of their psychological defences. The impact of this upon ourselves is potentially shattering . . .

Only potentially, however. Just as drama protects us from total involvement in someone else's agony, it also distances us from their utter discomfiture. Certainly we can be extremely embarrassed on their behalf and, if the experience is vivid enough to penetrate our own defences against embarrassment we may carry the feeling with us to the extent of its actually affecting our own attitudes towards people trapped in situations which expose their vulnerability. In real life other people's embarrassment embarrasses us as well. It has this contagious effect because we feel that it must be our fault they feel the way we do, it must be something we ourselves have said or done which has produced this effect. As the spectators of a play, however, we are absolved from this kind of responsibility, being in no way to blame for whatever may be happening to cause the character's discomfiture. In this case, all we feel is sympathy for people who are going through the kind of situations we ourselves find so very familiar, coupled with a certain understandable relief that it is all happening to them rather than to us.

Comedies are mainly about embarrassment, which is why we find them funny. Just as tragedy gives us permission to weep, so comedy and farce encourage us to laugh, there being nothing quite so amusing as self-confidence made to look ridiculous, particularly if we can reassure ourselves that these are, after all, not *real* people, are they? Real people's embarrassment is not nearly as funny; which is why we go to greater lengths to distance comic characters than tragic ones.

Television illustrates this well by taking ordinary people, non-actors, and using the theatricality which is inseparable from any kind of presentation to transform them into performers, so that now their embarrassment may be, quite literally, enjoyed at a distance. Seen like this, the notion of 'reality television' is deceptive, as no television which involves direction and editing may properly be described as 'reality'. Any kind of conscious presentation of human behaviour or experience in which the subjects concerned are specially arranged to produce a cathartic effect or encourage one to emerge when a select group of people – in this case the television audience – are looking in the right direction, is drama, and cannot avoid being so. Drama is what you do with your material, not what your material is, or even what it itself intends to be. Whatever it may say about itself, *Big Brother* is closer to *A Midsummer Night's Dream* than to any objective, dispassionate study of human experience – if such a thing could ever exist considering the depth of our own investment in whatever it may be that we are studying.

'Fly-on-the-wall' programmes are never what they claim to be. In other words, they are never entirely honest because they pretend that this kind of realism is actually achievable and that this is their aim in presenting the programme. Their main intention, however, is to create a particular kind of dramatic effect, on in which the observers (appropriately called 'viewers') may feel absolved from the necessity to take whatever it might be that they are eavesdropping on as in any way personally relevant to themselves. Hence they may feel entirely free to enjoy the embarrassment felt by the people whom they are observing, who know they are being secretly watched by immense numbers of people but who frequently seem to have forgotten the fact. Television of this kind pushes drama to its limits as it contrives to produce theatre without actors or audience by manipulating individuals into assuming these roles while claiming that such is not their intention. This cannot possibly be called theatre, they say, for where are the actors? But the audience knows, and so, most of the time, do the actors themselves, caught in a role from which it is not easy to escape, a drama which refuses to admit that it is 'only a play'.

Both types of theatre, the 'cavalcade' and the 'peep-show', cast those taking part, either as performers or audience members, as co-conspirators. Because neither is willing to admit their identity as actual drama, the agreement to join in the creation of an alternative reality where disbelief is not only suspended but genuinely shared, neither has the power to move us as plays do, so that we find ourselves able to forget in order to remember, to clear a space for feelings whose presence we need to acknowledge if we are to be at peace with ourselves and one another. Both are examples of what might be called 'trickster' theatre, requiring our belief yet withholding its own, exploiting our eagerness to collaborate and 'join the story', but leaving us unsatisfied because its use of deception gets in the way of its ability to point to any kind of recognisable truth.

Catharsis, however, depends on honesty. Cathartic drama is willing to admit its artificiality in defence of the authenticity of the feelings it portrays and the message it proclaims. The most basic theatre of all, conversational drama of the kind explored by Goffman and Scheff, aims at showing and sharing experience by involving us imaginatively with each other's meanings in order to bring us into relationship with one another.

"We were all just sitting there, and I turned round and thought,
   why not?"
"So what did you do?"
"I jumped right in, didn't I?"
"I bet you made a splash, all right!"

The fragment of dialogue has no significance in itself, as itself; we need more information, particularly about the people concerned: the person speaking, whoever is listening, the ones who are being talked about. I overheard it and it stuck in my mind long enough to be given as an example here. At the time it seemed to conjure up the vivid picture of something quite specific, an important incident in an unknown drama, nothing to do with me, but definitely important to the person talking – and to the listener, drawn into the story and obviously wanting to hear more. Both would have been irritated to know that someone else was listening to their private conversation. Dramatic it may have been, but not really intended to be public.

This is where theatre originates, in the conversational sharing of personal experience made vividly dramatic in order to convey immediacy. The aim is to communicate truth, something which really happened, by arranging it to best effect and presenting it as a dramatic scenario. In the case given here, the people involved in the incident may certainly have been 'sitting there' – but there was no 'turning round' or 'jumping in', although the person listening to the narrative finds no difficulty in suspending his or her disbelief in order to extend the dramatic metaphor: "I bet you made a splash."

This is not to say that, on occasion, we do not heighten reality in order to convince someone of something which we ourselves know to be untrue in order to put something across. We are usually aware that such is our intention. Almost without noticing it, however, we use the same technique to validate an experience we have actually had, or to make a point which we really believe to be true – to 'get something across'. Conversational theatre is available for both purposes. All the same, it works best for us when we set out to communicate something we really want to share, because then it has the ring of truth. Even at this mot rudimentary level, drama requires the pledge of mutuality which is genuine and authentic.

CHAPTER EIGHT
BELIEVING

There is a connection between the way some animals learn to perform tasks and the way people share experiences with one another. I have been arguing in this book that the similarity consists in the interior organisation of experience which holds elements of perception together along interior lines of organisation, as connected sequences, each of them distinguishable because it is identified as a sequence as distinct from a process. In other words, it has a beginning and an end whose function is to give perceptual cohesion to whatever occurs between them; it is this which allows them to function as percepts, distinguishable from the stream of consciousness, and capable of organisation into objects of perception which may be differentiated and consequently allied to other objects. The end of such a sequence is the crucial point in its emergence *as* a sequence; its assertion at some point in the ongoing process has a reflexive power to organise, balance and hold together the elements from which it emerged.

All this, of course, is arguing backwards, using a model of human communication to do so. We separate the things we want to say, but it is only because of an ongoing process of thinking (and feeling, of course) that we can say them at all. We interrupt them at points where the act of intervention would allow the separated section to stand by itself, so that we can manage to say at least part of what we mean. Then, like the cat who has manage to find the way out of the box, we have arrived at a sequence of events which is recognisably a sequence and can be used as such for the purpose we have in mind, which in this case is to say what we mean.

The notion of meaning as an expression of purpose, so that something may be seen as having it if in some way it contributes to its construction, is fundamental to the way that we communicate with one another. This is so whether or not we use language

– verbal language, that is – or not. We extend our meanings into sentences because we are not satisfied that what we want to say does really mean what we want it to until we have constructed a sentence round it. The experience of attaining communicable meaning and that of expressing it are one and the same, whether we address ourselves or someone else; in either case we are involved in construction, in putting things together to arrive at what is recognisable as belonging together.

To communicate personal meaning, either to ourselves or one another, we involve ourselves in learning, playing and imagining. These are all activities dependent on a sequence of elements, none of which makes sense apart from the others, or outside the order which is intrinsic to the whole and is able to give it a specific identity and purpose. Learning and playing, like other more obviously instrumental activities, require their sequences to be memorised in advance, while imagining is able to invent its own, whether or not they are intended to remain in the memory. In works of art we see both these things happening, as something devised and constructed receives the ability to image forth an imaginative life over which it has no strict control.

In every case the move to communicate presents us with an example of ordering where the successive elements fall retrospectively in place, as communication occurs and not before. According to this paradigm, learning is communication with oneself before it becomes any kind of message to someone else. As such it is always the completion of a process, the end-point in a progression, a journey which passes through various stages before arriving at its destination and is only recognisable in retrospect as a journey in terms of its connecting links, as the relationship between the stages reveal itself as the progressive realisation of the intention to communicate meaning, as balance, purpose, a sense of achievement.[67]

Each communication-journey itself signals and establishes the possibility of communicating, so that endings invite new beginnings; they do this because each successful project has cleared a space for the next, an opportunity for a new exercise in departure and arrival which will be taken up by those involved in the form of a response to the previous one. When this happens on the part of another person, the sharing of information can take place – either formally, as when a politician is heckled or a lecturer asks for questions, or informally in dialogue or conversation.

In all this, the signal itself plays a crucial role. It not only tells us when to join in, but how to do so, suggesting what sort of response is being asked for. We need to know, or at least to be able to guess, the personal and social circumstances in which the communication is being offered. Sometimes the message itself will tell us what we need to know; but not always. As we were saying earlier, we have to be aware of the kind of message it is, the spirit in which it is being offered, because this will influence our response in ways which may turn out to be decisive. For example, it is not always easy to judge whether a statement is rhetorical or whether we are supposed to reply to it; and there is the whole question about *how* things are said: the words chosen, the tone of voice used, which may apply to written as well as spoken messages; facial expression, use of gesture, posture, volume and speed of verbal delivery, even the mood or attitude of mind of the people delivering and receiving the message – whether they are themselves personally involved in the matter in hand, or simply bored by it.

What might be called 'the subjective context of messages which claim to be objective', in the sense of literal, is the deciding factor in the communication of meaning between and among people. In messages involving human beings it is impossible to say what the person delivering the message intends to be received by whomever is listening without taking into account who they are, where they are, and how they are listening. As we have seen in this book, nowhere is the truth more clearly apparent than in drama and theatre.

The questions asked by drama are always rhetorical in the sense that they assume our assent to their being asked – and our permission for them to be asked in this way. This way of doing things may not request a verbal response – not during the course of the play, that is – but it depends almost entirely on receiving a response which is signalled in other ways:

No matter how terrified I feel when I'm standing in the wings waiting to go on, or even if I'm feeling quite ill and think I may actually faint when I'm on stage, as soon as I put a foot on, everything's different. A great tide of warmth hits me. It's like jumping into the sea when the sun has warmed it up.[68]

The actor quoted above did not offer any explanation for the "great tide of warmth". For him it was enough that it happened and that it went on happening – which, he said, was why he went on being an actor. The warmth is the sensation which audiences communicate to actors or to anyone who enters the world which they, the audience, and the play with its cast of actors, are co-creating; and by entering this world becomes a participant of it. Or, if you prefer, an actor in it.

This actor's testimony, backed up by that of countless others both professional and amateur, is the most striking evidence available of the suspension of disbelief which allows us to enter the world which, by investing it with imaginative truth, we have voluntarily undertaken to share; and world in which cognitive and affective barriers to sharing have been deliberately transcended.

It is generally accepted that we share our imaginative life more freely than other ways we have of encoding information about our experiences. People who might be wary of communicating any information about what they really think and feel about life, so that they retreat into themselves if asked to give a considered opinion about something or other which they feel concerns them at a deep personal level, will quite willingly describe an imaginary situation concerning some fictional character. They will tell and listen to stories. They will enjoy watching TV dramas about situations they feel are very like their own; and the use of theatrical improvisations based on shared problems is a standby of therapeutic drama. When other ways into mutual acceptance stay closely guarded, the imagination-gate stands open.

Nevertheless its presence must not be taken for granted, but should always be clearly marked. Theatre signals its intentions more clearly than any other form of make-believe, telling us quite clearly that we are welcome to come in and make ourselves at home, so long as we are willing to bring our imaginations with us. The responsibility for doing this is ours. We think of it as make-believe and it is we ourselves, working in concert, who do the making. No-one makes us do it.

In fact we do it for pleasure. We are all well acquainted with imaginative experiences which are painful, some of which have stayed with us for a long time, haunting our imaginations, recurring time after time in our dreams. Perhaps some of our experiences of plays have been like that; perhaps if we go to see a play or offer to take part by playing an actual role in one, something like that will happen again because plays are able to revive things which have been safely laid to rest, so they obviously have a powerful effect on presences we know to be still lurking in our lives, waiting for the chance to jump out on us. A play would be the ideal opportunity, particularly seeing that plays involve us in other people's lives; so that we are distracted from the need to regulate feelings we have about our own . . .

But we go all the same, even though we know what we are letting ourselves in for. Or think we know, because no experience of allowing oneself to become involved in a play ever turns out to be exactly what we thought – or feared – it would be. How could it be? Even though the stories of plays may be familiar to us and the range of basic plots rather more restricted than we assumed it to be, the play itself is always different because the people in it are engaged in bringing it to life in a new way – and that includes everyone in the audience, 'resisters' and 'fellow-travellers' alike. This cannot avoid being so, because we are all different people, and plays, as well as reminding us of the things we share, also liberate the sense of our own individuality – which is exactly the gift we find ourselves moved to share with others in the expectation of being refreshed by the experience!

Drama is always a medium for imaginative sharing, as we use it to involve ourselves in a world whose fascination lies in its ability to set us free from our pre-occupation with ourselves. Theatre expands this experience by including us within the company of others engaged in the same project, making it hard to escape the conclusion that we have more in common with one another than each of us, in other circumstances would be likely to admit. In the theatre, we are all occupied with our own unique versions of the same range of feelings. The openness is the same, however; and this is what we have in common. The theatre accepts this willingness, and promises us that it will indeed be rewarded. After all, it is a gift of *trust*.

I realise that this may appear to be an idealistic view of what actually happens in theatres. Any area of life which intends to be inspirational falls short at least as often as it succeeds in its aim. I have myself worked in several theatres and taken part in many plays where the main aim seemed to be the manipulation of the audience. I have worked with actors who would have looked askance if anybody were to suggest that their job was to involve an audience rather than simply impress it with their skill in appearing to believe in the character they are playing. I have also been privileged to act alongside those who do genuinely believe in the truth of what is being created on stage between the audience and themselves.

The best performances I have taken part in, either as an actor or as a member of the audience, have always been like that; which after all is not surprising, there being more to art than showing off.[69] Acting is a mask to shelter behind, but the actors who appear to need this kind of protection, who in their life off-stage lack self-confidence so that they might be expected to use theatre as a way of pretending to be braver and more assertive than they can ever manage to be when they are 'being themselves'; these actors are the ones who take us by the hand and lead us into the reality of the person whom they are playing and through this into the reality of that person's world. These actors do gain confidence by taking on a role, but it is the confidence which belongs to stepping out to meet an accepting audience. In no way is it simply a desire to hide. Who could hide in so exposed a position? No 'characterisation' is ever tough enough to disguise the urge to seek safety, without this gift of the audience's acceptance. As I hope to have shown in this book, there is very much more to theatre than the impulse to hide coupled with the temptation to spy. For one thing, these are intensely private emotions – and theatre is anything but private.

An actor writes:

> It seems to me that playing to an audience of say 1000 people I am
> playing to different characters, different backgrounds, different
> hopes and dreams – and yet there are moments when all these
> things seem to vanish and yet become one: one with the author;
> one with your fellow actors and one with your audience.[70]

I have quoted these words before when I have been writing
about theatre, and I repeat them here because, of all the testi-
monies about acting which I have ever received, this is not only
the most moving but also the most profoundly truthful. Intrinsic
to theatre is a unifying power which is unequalled elsewhere. The
spiritual force which it generates calls to mind religious ritual;
and yet there is a difference, because those who attend religious
ceremonies already share a particular way of looking at life, a
weltanschauung which binds them spiritually together. In an
important sense, they are all, metaphorically speaking, looking in
a single direction so that each has the same expectations of what
is likely to take place. In religious ceremonies those taking part
already know the plot of the drama which is to be enacted. This
is far from the case in theatre, where even the most familiar story
may be changed in its presentation, and most plays aim deliberately at taking us somewhere unexpected: "Where should this
music be?"[71]

The actor goes on:

> The soul, the essence of ourselves, is the only thing we have in
> common. I believe it is the only thing that everyone can experi-
> ence at the same moment.

The actor's part in this is crucial, symbolising the way theatre
itself works:

> The actor must transmit from the stage the great gestures of the
> human soul and show them, and not himself, to the spectator. In
> order to experience this oneness, I have to get out of the way.[72]

Obviously this transparency, which is a willingness to allow the
meaning of the role to shine through in unison with that of the

play, each reflecting the other, is not compatible with any kind of compulsion on the part of either. The actor's transparency acts as catalyst, transforming the play as written into the experience of an actual encounter of persons which the author had in mind, so that this imagined world can take flesh. In the play as performed, actors and audience encounter one another in a willing acceptance of a truth that emerges between and among.

This is tough imagination, giving rise to an experience which lasts. The willingness to embark on this shared journey is borne out by a willingness to acknowledge the experience in retrospect. We do not simply enter the world of the play and then promptly forget where we have been, as happens in hypnosis, another example of disbelief willingly suspended. In drama willingness means what it says. What is required here is not capitulation but consent, a handing over of autonomy on both sides, resulting in an experience to be assimilated not dismissed as irrelevant. We do not escape into a place where there is no need to think or feel, a time when life's pressures are simply cancelled out; life under such conditions would not qualify as life, and we would have the greatest difficult imagining ourselves there . . .

What we can imagine, however, is a world where the oppositions which characterise our lives – love and hate, strength and weakness, confidence and insecurity, sense and nonsense, belonging and exclusion, despair and hope – and in this case imagination and reality – are held in balance. This is the reality which stays with us when we leave the theatre, affecting the way we relate to the world outside. The success of theatre is to be measured by what we ourselves carry away from it – the balance of pity and fear which is catharsis.

CHAPTER NINE

CONSENTING

The Wedding-Guest sat on a stone
He cannot choose but hear
And thus spake on that ancient man
  The bright-eyed Mariner.[73]

The Ancient Mariner shows no mercy- He requires not simply attention, but a total surrender. The story he is about to tell leaves no room for scepticism, as if this were a gentleman's agreement to share an imaginative experience transfixed by the Mariner's "glittering eye", the Wedding Guest has no option but to believe. As of course he does, de-parting from the encounter

A sadder and a wiser man.

And so do we, if we have paid attention to what Coleridge's genius has to offer. The terms of our engagement are somewhat different, of course; our acceptance of the story is free rather than forced, as we have undertaken to co-operate with the author and swap our own eyes for those of the Mariner, at least while we are reading the poem, that is – and such is the power of shared imagination, perhaps even afterwards as well. In this case the work of art demonstrates the contrast between willingness to believe which has been freely given, and the rigorous demands which may be imposed on us once we have crossed this particular threshold. Once inside the poem we move "like one that hath been stunned." Having once agreed to take part we find ourselves gripped as if we ourselves were characters in the drama. This is what Coleridge does simply by writing a poem and inviting us to share it with him.

But it must be a willing sharing, otherwise the magic will not work. Certainly we have to believe, but our belief must be freely given, because the operation whereby we hold separate worlds in a creative tension without permitting either to dominate depends on our allowing a special kind of relationship to exist between them. The two worlds are not parallel, being conceived as opposites; as challenge and security, threat and reassurance; as safety and danger, joy and sadness, homecoming contrasted with banishment and exile, as darkness and light; as Heaven and Hell. Within the experience of art, contrast is perceived as balance and balance as *interchange*, the overall resolution of conflict wherever it is encountered "La poésie vicu" says Victor Hugo[74] "la poésie complète, est dans l'harmonie dè contraires"

This is resolution not reduction. Conflict must be recognized before harmony may be achieved. The message of art, and particularly of theatre is that these conflicts give way once they are faced; and that this may be done most effectively in the sphere in which they are able to exert their authority over us, the realm of the imagination. The resolution of conflict depends on its recognition. So much is obvious. What is not so immediately apparent is the positive value of allowing them to assume the living form of a work of art in which they can be clearly seen: in which we can let ourselves see them clearly.

If we are willing, that is. Unlike the Wedding Guest, we ourselves are free to walk away, in order to be able to get up next morning refreshed by a good night's sleep, untroubled by what we have been forced to contemplate. It is art's privilege to be ignored, and ours to do the ignoring. We are entirely free to reject the possibility of a transforming experience, and the greater the pressure which may be put on us the less the experience qualifies as artistic. For the Wedding Guest the Mariner's tale is a first hand experience, as indeed it was for the Mariner himself; neither have any need to "suspend their disbelief". For us, however, it is otherwise. We are perfectly at liberty to be bored, incredulous, derisive, or simply to refuse to waste our time being any of these things. The images embedded in it are amongst the most powerful ones in any poem in the English language; but this judgment is only viable to those who have read it, and whether we decide to do so is entirely up to us; or at least we will receive them more powerfully if this is the case, but even if, as in so many cases the poem is 'required reading' we are unlikely ever to forget them.

All the same we will remember them most vividly if we ourselves have chosen to read the poem, and better still if we have stumbled on it by chance; much in the same way as the cat backed on to the lever and discovered the way out of its box. The element of discovery is important. We are more likely to find ourselves returning to things which we associate with surprised delight, even if custom has taken the edge off the surprise for us. Those who have benefited from suspending disbelief, who have been enriched by the experience, are the most willing to try it out again. They will keep coming back even when for some reason of mood or circumstance, on their own part or that of the work itself, the task of joining in the game of believing has seemed more difficult to achieve – has in fact become a task, rather than a release, something to be endured rather than enjoyed. But even then imagination is very likely to seize the opportunity to exercise the life, the irrepressible vitality, which is its own and which refuses to be denied; and when it comes it does so as the willingness to be involved, to take part.

Art and willingness go together. From this point of view, art itself is structured willingness. Herein lies its importance for transforming lives. The value of any work of art lies not in that it exists but that it has no need to do so. Plays like any other form of artistic expression, are optional. No-one forces us to take seriously this balancing act between worlds. We tend to confuse liking theatre with actually having to do it, a state of mind which is more excusable in cats than people. The benefits of taking part are obvious, for here are the things about being human which disturbs us so much, in a form able to resolve the discord and restore a sense of harmony and purpose. If we can assent to the way in which they are presented to us, we can take their truth into our lives and use it as our own. If not, then we can simply say, no harm done.

If we ourselves are wiser through the Wedding Guest's having to believe, this is not because we are forced to be, but because we choose to be. We have learned that to ignore it is to miss an opportunity we have been offered and have benefited on previous occasions from having taken up. The testimony of those subjected to intensive interrogation bears witness to the fact that there are other ways of persuading us that things are actually other than we had supposed them to be, particularly if the physical and psychological distress caused by our efforts to hold on to our perceptions of a situation becomes more than we can bear. We are immediately reminded of political prisoners who are persuaded to reverse their opinions about their captors as a result of being tortured or suffering sensory deprivation – which of course, amounts to the same thing – such treatment having activated the desire to seek release by training oneself first to understand, then actually to assimilate someone else's point of view thus making acquiescence to their demands not just feasible but actually praiseworthy.

Social psychologists point out that this way of solving our personal problems is not as rare as we might think. In fact it is extremely common.[75] If enough pressure is put on us, we may well begin to distrust our own judgment, so that, before very long we find ourselves looking round for ways of revising our interpretation of the situation; perhaps ours is not the only reasonable way. After all, it has to be admitted that, from their point of view, theirs is reasonable, too, or at least they honestly believe it to be so. All this is very natural, and ought not to be regarded as evidence of weak mindedness or a tendency to vacillate. On the contrary being able to see one another's point of view is the very foundation of human relationship. Any attempt at understanding how theatre works depends primarily on this fact about us.

But this is a process of working through, rather than the instantaneous decision to trust our imagination described by Coleridge, which is a leap of faith rather than any kind of negotiated agreement. We do not debate within ourselves as to whether we are willing to be willing. There is no element of exertion in the way Coleridge describes our enjoyment of poetry or Victor Hugo writes about theatre. Our imaginations respond willingly to the way we are addressed by the theatrical event. Despite all the paraphernalia involved in presentation – the writing of scripts, auditions, rehearsals, stage lighting and sound, costume and make-up, talent itself – the happening is simple and immediate, nothing more than an act of recognition. These other things can help but they can also get in the way. Imagination freely responds to the invitation to take itself seriously, aware that in the ordinary course of events it is only rarely given the chance; suddenly, without taking thought, imagination agrees to be seen in public in order to show just what it is capable of doing. No wonder it is so interested in joining in with whatever may be going on!

The "willing suspension of disbelief". Other things conspire to shake our confidence in the world we depend on, which we have learned to regard as the only kind of world which may reasonably be cast in the role of truth-bearer, but they all involve the limitation of our freedom. Only art has the ability to expand our reality instead of contradicting it, to liberate rather than constrain our awareness of others and ourselves without recourse to altering the chemical constitution of our brains or putting our central nervous systems into overload. Only art can enlarge our experience in the direction of greater balance and the reduction of intrapsychic disharmony in the shape of psychological conflict. Art which encourages us to take its linguistic code seriously enough to pay attention to the messages it communicates, to trust in its ability to furnish us with answers to our problems which we will be able to use.

The therapeutic value of art lies in its power to speak to our pain without becoming snarled up in our defensiveness.[76] It cannot do this unless we believe in it; that is unless we abrogate our own power to 'demythologise' it. Susanna Langer[77] has distinguished between the extended symbolism of story telling, where the story itself is the metaphor for the presence of a wider, more generalised purpose than the mere recording of events –'discursive' symbolism through which meaning reveals itself in the unfolding of the tale – and 'presentative' symbolism, where a single image brings an entire world into view. The play's story leads us more deeply into the action whereby we give ourselves to the process of realizing, making real, something we know to be a fiction. The play itself however, through its existence as an "integrating focus"[78] speaks to us as presence not process, a living symbol which in itself has no extension, but only depth. Because it is both place and story, theatre combines both kinds of symbol, a source of unity for our divided experience.

This being so, plays which set out to instruct rather than involve us completely miss the point, which is that, in itself, theatre is not, and cannot be straightforwardly instrumental. It can't be used to do one thing and avoid doing anything else. From this point of view theatres are useless places. Indeed they are places to go to in order to be useless. We may find a use for ourselves there, but the place itself has no purpose at all otherwise. No one goes there because they have to. Even actors cannot be forced to act; at least, not to act *well*.[79] Perhaps this is why theatre is commonly thought of as entertainment, pleasant but pointless, with no strings attached, a way of filling in time which we have often enjoyed.

This is theatre as escapism, there to take your mind off things. Pooh's "warm and shady spot"[80] Certainly it can be this, just as it can be all sorts of other things too, its principal, underlying characteristic being its optional nature. It may function as a clinic or a consulting room, a class-room or a lecture theatre, a clubhouse or a church, but it will not ever actually feel like any of these things. What then does it feel like? Like an extraordinary location of some kind, a special place, a world of its own, but without any suggestion that here we are protected against life and the things which happen in it; the painful feelings produced by it, which scar its fabric and throw it off balance.

In theatre we entertain this awareness and willingly acknowledge these feelings. Willingness here turns out to be crucial. Willingness, that is, not eagerness. We are privileged in these circumstances to be able to relate to the demands of our own humanity in a different way, by acknowledging their presence instead of guarding ourselves against them; at once protected and exposed by the action of co-creation which is able to deliver us from an interiority which has become burdensome into a cultural reality where the need for interchange is not only clearly recognized, but symbolically consummated.[81] The language is corporate rather than private; co-creation speaks by the shape of its overall action, not by the significance of individual gestures, making sense by means of the way it organizes its own world.

This characteristic of being 'a world of its own', detached from the rest of life, a self enclosed workshop for living kept separate from the normal conditions affecting the material it is dealing with, is usually associated with ritual behaviour, where ritual is defined as action performed only with reference to itself, having no connection with its purposes outside the ritual context. Both animals and human beings 'use' this kind of ritual; Professor Thorndike's cat, for instance learned very quickly that what worked outside the box worked very differently inside, where everything had to be done in a particular order. Outside the box all his usual procedures produced their usual results; here in the box, however they only worked in association with one another, losing their individual effectiveness in the process of doing so.

Some students of corporate human ritual have drawn attention to this self-referential quality which has no intrinsic structural reference.[82] By this they mean that the principle governing this way of communicating meaning differs from the way we usually talk about things. This is not surprising, because ritual is the way we express things we find it hard to talk about, things which don't fit the kind of sense we depend on being able to make of conflict and confusion.[83] They are the language of difference; and insofar as they resemble plays, this is the aspect of theatre which they share – theatre as related to but detached from ordinary experience. Theatre as an *interruption* of life.

The 'structural reference' of plays as of corporate rituals, is to human non-communication, the unthinkable collapse of the ways we make sense of life. This is built into their structure, along with the impossible return of meaning – new meaning, not something following from what went before. Meaning which happens out of the blue. Ordinary sense, the way we go about anticipating things is no longer any use; it is precisely this which got in the way of genuine renewal, so that it has had to be stopped and dealt with as efficiently as possible. We may laugh or weep at a play, but its action must involve some kind of reversal of our expectations in order for it to be a play at all.[84]

Both theatre and ritual speak the language of discontinuity. They have to do so in order to be the bearers of a message about a greater continuity, revealed in terms of the collapse of the former state of affairs, the one presented in the rite or the play itself. In a sense, then, their message is self-contained. However it possesses a wider function than this because of the power it has to resonate with those of us living in an altogether different world; different because it is shown as dramatically separated from our own. We may identify with it but we remain separated from it. As we have seen in this book it is this separation which draws us in, this difference which encourages us to enter. But it is the scenario which is set apart, not the characters whom we recognize as sharing our nature. These people in the play-world who act as our representatives, and whose experiences chime with our own.

Hence the ability of both rite and theatre to speak to things we experience as our own failures to make sense. They do this because of their structure as well as their content, or rather because of the way that their structure presents their content. Therapeutic drama aims at creating a setting in which intense experiences of living, presented fictionally in drama, may themselves act as learning points for those involved. The drama itself is self-contained, and its language officially refers only to the characters taking part, but its reference is really much wider and its function within human society infinitely more important.[85]

By stressing entertainment value and managing not to remind ourselves of the emotional cost of taking seriously a medium which is capable of actualising such pain, so many memories we have trained ourselves not to dwell on, we run the risk of under-valuing theatre by seriously misunderstanding the way it works: the way it works *on us*. To say this, however, is to ignore art's ability to present truth – even painful truth – as a kind of game.

Understandably we are more willing to play games than face truths. At the same time, the games we most enjoy playing are those which it has cost some effort to win. No game must be too easy to play, not if we are to feel it was worth playing, and the ones which we remember, which stand out in our memory are those which we thought ourselves in real danger of losing, if we were able to contemplate such a thing. In such cases, it is the memory of having avoided failure which sticks in our minds even more than the satisfaction of the success itself. The only way we can lay this ghost is by making sure that whatever the result may be in terms of actual winning we shall have done our best; and this, in game playing terms, is the real measure of failure or success. If we have striven our hardest, then we have come through honourably.

And so it is with theatre. We sense that here in this game of pretending, where we undertake to keep the rules of an alternative reality – a different reality but the same rules – we are liable to find ourselves identifying with those whose world this is, and who will be liable to suffer in consequence. We will laugh with them, but we will also weep, the main purpose of this alternative reality being to draw attention to the way in which these two activities, tears and laughter, actually relate to each other in both of these worlds, our own and the one we are opting to take part in. We are willing to play this particular game but not too willing, and so we find ourselves playing an even more familiar one, that of pretending not to have to take serious things seriously enough to be committed to caring about them in any way or to any degree which would cause us distress. We are willing to be entertained, or even if such a thing is really necessary, perhaps a little moved, but that is as far as it goes.

What we certainly do not want to be is harrowed. Perish the thought! And yet, at a somewhat deeper level, this is in fact why we have come. When we say that we want to be taken out of ourselves, this is actually what we *do* want: to laugh and to cry, mourn and rejoice, wail and be reconciled. We want these things and have such difficulty in allowing ourselves to have them. Our violence in longing reflects our determination to guard ourselves against giving in. At the risk of sounding dramatic, they are gestures of the soul which we find alarming, frank and outspoken, signifying as they do a degree of commitment to being fully alive, fully human, that we are unwilling to embark upon. But it is drama's job to be dramatic, and to be it on our behalf and for our sake.

In giving us permission to express things about ourselves of which we find it easier not to admit any ownership theatre says something like this: If these things are yours, then have them. Take them to yourselves. If they are not yours, amuse yourselves at the expense of those you see behaving in ways you yourself find ridiculous, or reprehensible, or pathetically inadequate. No one here is forcing you to admit participation in ways of thinking and feeling, acting and reacting which you yourself perceive as alien to your own experience, the person you know yourself to be; but if on the other hand when you allow yourself to be drawn into what is going on here because it reminds you of yourself and starts you feeling as if you yourself were actually one of the people involved, then theatre's purpose in achieving self knowledge, rooted as it is in the experience of human vulnerability, is nourished by a more intense awareness of our relationship with others.

The feelings theatre brings to the surface have been disguised and kept hidden because of their power to destroy our repose. Artaud was surely right to bring this to our attention. By disguising them as fictional, we divert their force elsewhere, making them seem less dangerous; but the emotions themselves remain, their immediacy lessened but their nature preserved by the action of setting them at a distance by inventing a world for their containment. Our attempts to control them have the effect of increasing their power to appear before us as themselves, as in their immediate state they arouse a defensiveness able to disguise their presence much more effectively than the artificiality of theatre – our awareness, that is, of its artificial nature – could ever succeed in doing.

But this power is expressed in the reassuring form of a game, depending on the willing participation of those taking part. Because it has all the force of a presentational metaphor this game must somehow be approached with caution. It cannot simply be rushed into. The revelation it enshrines depends entirely on the way we approach it. We must let it speak to us in its own language without making demands of our own . In turn the demands it makes on us are, to begin with, only slight; anything more demanding will be tackled later on, and we will be provided with the wherewithal to do this when the time comes. In the meantime, however, all that is required of us is the willingness to co-operate by doing our best to take this- particular game seriously – which means of course being willing to abide by its basic rule, that of treating the reality it comprises as an authentic one, to be trusted and not simply 'seen through'.

Theatre, then, is a gentlemen's (or ladies') agreement rather than a contract of any kind. What it definitely is not, is a process; although the play itself is constructed by means of the relationship created by its individual sections or 'movements'. The play itself is a system, but its identity as drama, and its actual presentation as theatre is entirely a-systematic, depending on our willingness to co-operate in using our imagination to give flesh to the bones of an idea. If there is a process involved, it is that of translating a private language into one which is shared by others and agreeing with them that this is in fact what we intend to do. The agreement itself, however, is freely given, freely made.

Those who write about theatre commonly use the phrase "willing suspension of disbelief" as if it had been by Coleridge specifically for the purpose of describing the terms of engagement between actors and audiences on one hand, and on the other, an individual actor and the role she or he is playing. In fact as we saw earlier, there is no direct reference to theatre at all in the way Coleridge uses the words. They were written about poetry itself and the imaginative world it inhabits, where nothing is proclaimed or perfected and meanings are shared rather than transmitted, the distance to be covered being that between the written word and the receiving mind and heart. Certainly the notion of performance is absent unless we ourselves introduce it, which is never the case with drama, even drama which is read rather than acted. Words take the place of actors, mediating a relationship which is more private, less determined to be brought to public attention.

Nevertheless it remains the same relationship, the artistic event in which the acknowledgment of distance summons us to exchange experiences of selfhood with one another. The fact that Coleridge is describing poetry and we use his words to explain theatre draws attention to the quality of our own receptiveness when we approach drama, in either the written or its acted form. Simply being present is not enough. It is what we bring with us that matters, the attitude which will allow a play to be theatre or an arrangement of words on a page to reach out to us as poetry.

What happens in art of any kind does so because we give it permission.

Permission is all that is needed. It is our gift to art, which must receive it in order to exist. Basically we are not required to do anything else, but we must be ready to allow the work of art to speak, and agree to listen to its message. Because artistic communication happens within the dimension of imagination, willingness to take it seriously involves abandoning the urge to take everything literally, deciding, at least for the time being, not to listen to a voice whose authority we are unused to questioning. Seeing we are all so used to valuing suspicion as a paramount requirement for our own safety, being asked to pay more attention to fiction than what we usually think of as fact represents more of a challenge than we might suppose. Perhaps it is harder nowadays than it used to be; all the same, this is something which can never have come easily to human beings, so that even in more trusting times people may have felt nervous about it.

But thinking about it is not what we're asked to do. Thinking about it is what we are asked to *suspend*. It is not a question of convincing ourselves that we believe something to be real despite the evidence that this is in fact not the case, although it turns out that we can go a long way towards doing this, if we really make the effort, and the way to believing in the new truth has been cleared by the expertise of others who are adept at this kind of deception. It is not really about making an effort at all, because it is something we discover we want to do. However hard we try to disguise the fact, playing like this, co-operating in make-believe, is something we enjoy doing. It is a release and it gives us release, freeing us from the nets we ourselves have spun – and been caught in – and opening up areas of humanness, our own and others, which we are otherwise inhibited from entering. We possess the skill to do these things, but we need to be given permission to use it, it seems unreasonable to behave in ways which cannot be described as practical.

Theatre however cannot be reasonably described as a private aberration. Under such circumstances, taking part in dramas is officially held to be an acceptable way of behaving. Suspending our disbelief like this represents behaviour which is culturally conformist: one reason perhaps why we find ourselves so willing to do it. It is an available avenue of escape from the preoccupations and anxieties which are the terms of our ordinary involvement with one another and ourselves. But it is more than a need for distraction. It is something which holds within itself the promise of genuine fulfilment, and at some level we know this.

The desire to take part, to let ourselves become, in one way or another personally involved in the play is the same desire that we have to be fully involved in life, fully alive. We reach out for an opportunity to free ourselves from whatever stands in the way of this – things about ourselves, things about our relationships with one another. Theatre is a door held open for us. It is up to us to decide whether or not to obey the impulse to find out what lies beyond. This what theatre is in itself; something which is available for use. It must however be used in a certain way.

Theatre has to be treated in accordance with its own essential nature as an occasion for meeting, a promise of future revelations. If we regard it as this, it will lead on to more tangible results, reach more definite conclusions, but its essential nature is as opportunity. Our commitment to it must be to allow it a freedom which, bound by constraints regarding the nature of what should or should not be believed by rational people, we are not yet capable of enjoying. Our enthusiasm to take part should be tempered with discretion; we should understand how easy it would be to interfere with the new creation by our determination to hold on to a state of mind appropriate for other situations but almost certain to prove itself destructive in this setting. Theatre asks to be given a chance to be allowed to be itself, so that it can show us what it can do. We do not need to prove it, it will prove itself.

That is, it will do so if we let it. By the quality of our applause we register the intensity of our involvement. This is measured by our willingness to let the play speak, to believe in its right to do so; which, of course involves believing in the play itself being willing to accept its terms. As in the example given in Chapter 1, where the cat's dysfunctional behaviour was a necessary part of its gaining freedom, so for people who frequent theatres, either as audiences or actors, release takes place when practical ways of coping with reality have been jettisoned. Like the cat, we do it because it works for us, which is why, like the cat we enjoy doing it.

The difference is, or course, that unlike the cat we ask ourselves why! Why do we enjoy it? Or, in terms of the question I have asked so many times here, why are we so willing to do it? What does our willingness mean? Certainly the cat can be made to do a large part of the business of explaining the tendency we have to make up plays, and find ways of enjoying them together, by directing attention to the satisfaction of completed processes and the way that plays hang together and have to be lived through and not simply thought about in order to achieve their purpose for us. We would not expect cats to be capable of creating "a world of the imagination", certainly, but if they were they would certainly go there to play, cats being addicted to one kind of enjoyment or another; and they would be surprised and delighted by what they discovered, as Thorndike's cat was when he managed, once again, to find the way out of his box.

The cat enters the box again and again because of its satisfaction in escaping. Certainly this is one of the reasons for our own willingness to take on the make-believe of theatre. However the transition we must make is one in which the difference between the two environments is much more radical. Stated baldly, cats are not required to enter an imaginary box of their own making, but plays depend on us to give them their life, and the life which we bestow on them is of another kind altogether. For us the transition means standing back from one kind of reality in order to move across into another. It involves our being in a place where two realities meet. The 'disbelief' we must 'suspend' is in two opposing realities co-existing without one of them cancelling the other out: the reality of a world skilled in presenting illusion as truth, and that of the world created among us by this presentation, where truth transcends the way it has been delivered. Both of these must somehow be believed, so that neither may be forced on us, and they are held together in balance by those willing to accept that such a thing can be possible.

Art springs to life when opposites are allowed to exist in creative tension. In theatre these opportunities are not only ideas, but separate human realities, for as Shakespeare says, the play-house is a place where

> "Such as give
> Their money out of hope they may believe,
> May here find truth too."[85]

CONCLUSION

What happens in theatre does so between people. It is always difficult to tie down interpersonal processes to any stimulus-reinforcement paradigm; never more so, however, in drama and theatre, where imaginative sharing takes place in conditions arranged specifically for the purpose of examining a particular phenomenon which otherwise proves to be too elusive to be captured. It is not a case of finding a way of focusing on 'theatrical between-ness' by providing the appropriate experimental conditions for operationalising it; quite the opposite, in fact, for drama, in its expanded form as theatre, brings the phenomenon to our attention in the clearest way we could imagine by constructing a model of between-ness in which its various expressions can be examined under laboratory conditions – a laboratory designed for this particular phenomenon so that it can be studied.

An actor said. "Theatre is a camera with its lens turned inwards."[86] Theatres don't have to be buildings, as our minds when faced with the written text of a play imagine their own theatres and proceed to take it from there. The intangible, unmeasurable, abstract subject-matter – what actually happens between and among people – is realised not in itself, but in the way it shows itself to us. Theatre focuses on a space capable of creating relationship. The psychology necessary for understanding it is aesthetic, concerning the emergence of meaning from emotion: what can be experienced but not explained except in terms of the feelings and ideas it gives rise to and the actions it provokes. Its truth lies in its wholeness, and dividing it up for purposes of identification renders it incomplete and consequently deprives it of meaning. Theatre exists to preserve it intact.

Here are some of the things involved:

- Playing, imagining, learning; working towards meaning; balance, wholeness, reaching across to others; taking account of their otherness; sharing involvement with one another and the world; opening our interior universes to others in exchange; voyaging forth together as exchange becomes interchange; carrying back truth found on the journey; discovering the meaning of things encountered but not mastered (which is the purpose of imagination and the manifest reason for valuing it).
- Hesitating to dive in and finding we can swim; being intensely aware of the company of others yet not finding this intrusive or a distraction; being encouraged by their presence to open ourselves up to the transforming power of the imagination; trusting the metaphor and finding release in doing so – release, support and encouragement . . .
- Releasing the creativity we possess but are wary of using; allowing it the expression for which it yearns in the form of stories about ourselves and the world we are sharing; embodying it in dramas constructed for the purpose of sending out messages about truth which affect the practical business of day-to-day living.
- Inviting us to face things which terrify us – or would do if we had not shut them away so that they remain out of reach when we actually need them; creating the cathartic balance which alone is able to resolve the conflict stirred up in us by our characteristic ways of looking at life.
- Reminding us that hope and purpose are to be found in an image of relationship.

All these things belong to the drama which opens out for us when we agree together to suspend disbelief long enough to embrace the wholeness known otherwise in the form of fragments of a reality which contains us but itself remains elusive and ungraspable. What we see in the form of drama may not be the whole story, certainly; but for us the parts hold together, allowing us, like Thorndike's cat, to subscribe to it without having to destroy its unity.

POSTSCRIPT BY SIÂN PHILLIPS

Actors make up a small proportion of the people who take part in the event that is a Night Out at the Theatre. Because we are brightly lit and everyone else is in darkness, because (ideally) we are the ones talking and the others are sitting silently, we assume that we are in complete control. It stands to reason that to an extent, this is true. We know the words, we know the story, we know what effect the director had in mind and where this might coincide or differ from the author's intention, and why that might be. We are also privy to myriad scraps of information concerning what is occurring backstage. Does this knowledge give us control? Only partially. Whatever one's role, whatever ones connection with theatre it is very difficult to talk sensibly about performance.

An awful lot of nonsense is heard in the foyers of theatres. "Alright I suppose, if you like a great play" (this about a very well-written and acclaimed play). "Oh no, dearie. I don't think so" (this after one of those hugely appreciated star turns). I've heard myself saying "That was the Best/ Worst thing that has ever happened to me. I have to go and lie down."

The things we say in the feverish, pumped up atmosphere of the darkened wings bear even less examination. The most frequent question is "What are they like?" They. Have some eight hundred people assumed one identity? During a comedy which doesn't seem to be going as well as usual there will be a fretful "They're not laughing" and inevitably someone will say consolingly "But they're really listening." When the laughs are deafening we often remark that "They" are all gorgeous and can come again, ignoring the probability that at least a third of those darlings are bored stiff and longing for the interval. Conversely, on nights when They are horrid or hostile (or so we imagine because we missed our exit round) it's hard to remember that quite a lot of them might be having a grand old time and silently willing the play to go on for ever.

We talk in this fashion because we don't know exactly what it is that we are engaged on together. Sometimes we're scared. In the theatre things rarely go exactly to plan and nothing is quite the same two nights running. Each night at the same time we try to travel along a pre-arranged path but it pays to remember that we are dealing in uncertainties.

Like most actors I seldom talk about my job, aware that the more I say the less sense I make (there are some honourable exceptions). This is not because I'm particularly stupid but because, far from being someone in control I know I am someone involved in a mystery and because I have to do it every night I had best leave it that way. This is not to say that I am not curious and I often wonder over the things that take place within the four walls of the theatre. It certainly does not mean that others shouldn't try to work out the puzzle.

Sometimes I read a book about the theatre and not only do I not quite understand a good deal of it, I don't recognise the bits I do understand as being anything much to do with what I spend most of my life doing. I welcome Roger Grainger's book because, at the same time as he lays out explanations he recognizes the mystery. I like the idea that all of us, each night, enter into an agreement to share our experiences. I am aware that, as a member of the audience, the artifice of the situation – me sitting there watching people pretending to be someone else – makes me feel safe enough to confront truths I might not otherwise care to think about. When I say 'I am aware' I mean I recognise this as true but I had never before formulated it. In the same way, as I read it, I understand that a great deal of my satisfaction in the theatre derives from the fact that someone has imposed order on events – something so absent from my everyday life. I also have a feeling that it is true that, as actors, we are braver and go further than we are able easily to do in our own lives; but as I implied earlier I would like to be excused from enlarging on that. But Roger

Grainger is not so excused, and his book sheds welcome light on the unifying power of theatre – a power which, in my experience, is unequalled.

APPENDIX

MERELY PLAYERS

The setting is a large room in a community health centre. It is 7.25 p.m. A dramatherapy session is due to begin at 7.3 0 p.m. So far only two people have arrived, the therapist (Roger) and Simon, who is about 40 years old, and has recently been made redundant. Roger is doing his best not to appear anxious at the evident lack of support. *"Well, they said they wanted to come."* At 7.35 p.m. the door of the room opens and five more people come in. There are four women, two in their thirties, two ten years older, and a young man. *"We were waiting outside,"* says the young man. When everybody has taken their coats off Roger suggests that they say what their names are. This is the first session out of a course of ten.

They stand in a circle and say their names: Simon, Bruce, Gwen, Anna, Barbara, Louise, Roger. Nobody seems very sure of themselves. Roger surveys the group and realises that the ice needs to be broken.

ROGER: *Let's play some daft games to get used to one another.*
BARBARA: *Excuse me, I hope you don't mind, but I just came along with Louise. I'd like to stay on the side lines if you don't mind.*
ROGER: *I'll tell you what. This bit's only about names. If you get to something you don't like, you can drop out. O.K.?*

Barbara grins sheepishly and nods. Roger's name game consists in saying one's own name and then saying the name of the person to the left or right of oneself, who then has to do the same thing. Nobody knows which way this will go, and sometimes it just goes backwards and forwards. People begin to laugh at the battles arising from this. Bruce mentions another game,

'Grandmother's Footsteps'. This consists of creeping up and trying to steal a bunch of keys from in front of a blindfolded person. The group play this for a while, until everyone – including Barbara – has been blindfolded.

Everybody is a good deal more relaxed now.

ROGER: *What's it all about, do you think?*
SIMON: *Fooling about, if you ask me*
ANNA: *Getting people to relax.*
ROGER: *Well, it's certainly about people. This first session's about getting to know one another.*

He asks the group to divide up into pairs, choosing someone that they don't know as a partner. Barbara and Louise are allowed to be partners. The partners stand facing each other, with the palms of their hands almost touching. (*"So you can feel the warmth from the other person's palm."*) One person moves her or his hands while the other follows, as if reflections in a mirror. First one leads, then the other. Slowly, quickly, slowly again. Louise and Barbara turn out to be very skilful and move around the room mirroring each other. Then a game in which one turns away, while the other changes his or her appearance very slightly: *What's different about me?*

ROGER: *See if you can remember something about the other person so well, that you can say it as if it were you.*

Partners tell each other the history of the clothes they are wearing. Having done this, they report what they remember to the rest of the group in the following way.

GWEN: *I am Bruce (her partner) and I bought these shoes from my twin brother, etc. . . . .*

People find this role-reversal rather hard at first, and keep slipping into the third person (*"I am Louise, and she bought her jumper etc . . . "*) Once they have got used to it, most of the group find it fun. Even Barbara makes no move to back out . . .

Dramatherapy is not a way of using drama to teach behaviour, but a way of experiencing relationships which are presented by the dramatic process. In other words, the way people relate to one another is experienced and understood by means of the dramatic framework. I love it in the way that a swimmer loves the water. This is dramatherapy at its simplest – our feet haven't left the floor of the bath yet; we are still going through the motions, still scared to take the plunge.

Not entirely though. Even at this stage the experience of drama is beginning to give us buoyancy. As it is with anything to do with drama, it's a matter of courage and concentration. Nobody in the group thinks that he or she can act; and yet, in their own time and their own way, they are all taking part in the imaginative interchange of personal realities that is drama.

I have been a dramatherapist for more than twenty years now, working mainly in a psychiatric setting, It is very different from being an actor (although I still do some of that as well). I find myself working more as a facilitator, helping others to construct their own theatres from their own experience and their sense of life's meaning. Sometimes it is exciting, sometimes dull – but it is always authentic, never simply an opportunity for showing off. In this setting, the drama itself is the therapy, not simply an aid to therapy; it is the place of meeting and the meeting itself.

Because it combines structure (character, plot and presentation) and freedom (through the suspension of extra-dramatic reality), therapeutic drama is experienced as liberating by people oppressed by a restricted sense of themselves as independent persons – as in depression – or by the lack of an integrated self-image, as in schizoid awareness. Our plays are simple and crudely put together, our acting clumsy and self conscious, but it is our acting, our play. I seem to remember someone saying to me at RADA that, in theatre, it is truth that matters most. Human truth is what dramatherapy is about. Not far from Gower Street, after all.

NOTES

One LEARNING

1 Thorndike's experiment is described in D. E. Broadbent, *Behaviour* (1964), pp. 56, 57.

2 Perhaps we sometimes think of the mind, or parts of it, as a receptacle for containing information, memory being the source of future behaviour. Freud illustrates this in his description of the unconscious: "We have adopted the hypothesis of a psychological apparatus, extended in space, appropriately constructed, developed by the exigencies of life, which gives rise to the phenomena of consciousness only at one particular point and under certain conditions" (*An Outline of Psychoanalysis*, 1949, p. 65).

3 "If we speculate about the evolution of communication, it is evident that a very important stage . . . occurs when the organism gradually ceases to respond quite 'automatically' to the mood-signs of another and becomes able to recognise the sign as a signal . . . which can be trusted, falsified, denied, amplified, corrected and so forth." (Gregory Bateson, 'A Theory of Play and Fantasy', in *Steps to an Ecology of Mind*, 1973).

4 E. Goffman, *The Presentation of Self in Everyday Life* (Penguin, 1971). See also T. S. Scheff, *Goffman Unbound* (Paradigm, 2006).

5 See Scheff, *Goffman Unbound*, pp. 26–8.

6 I have been greatly influenced in all my thinking on this subject by Martin Buber, *I and Thou* (T&T Clark, 1966); *Pointing the Way* (Routledge, 1957); and also *Between Man and Man* (Collins, 1961).

7 S. Butler, *Hudibras*, pt. III, Ch. 3, line 547 (1678).

8 R. D. Laing, *The Divided Self* (Penguin, 1965), pp. 44ff.

9 *Ibid.*, p. 45: "The other's love is therefore feared more than his hatred, or rather, all love is sensed as a version of hatred."

Two TRUSTING

10 S. T. Coleridge, *Biographia Litteraria* (1817), ch. xiv. "He holds him with his glittering eye": The Mariner himself denies the Wedding Guest any chance to suspend disbelief willingly. In this case, disbelief is not an option.

11 See A. Gersie and N. King, *Storymaking in Education and Therapy* (Kingsley, 1990).
12 See S. H. Butcher, *A Commentary on Aristotle's 'Poetics'* (Dover, 1951).
13 See M. Buber (1957), p. 72.
14 See note 1.
15 T. J. Scheff, *Catharsis in Healing, Ritual and Drama* (California University, 1979), p. 13.
16 *Ibid.*, p. 60.
17 Shakespeare, *The Tempest*, Epilogue.

Three SHARING

18 See P. Brook, *The Empty Space* (1968); also M. Duggan and R. Grainger, *Imagination, Identification and Catharsis in Theatre and Therapy* (Kingsley, 1997), pp. 119–37.
19 See S. Kierkegaard, *Either/Or* (Princeton), p. 223: "For (he) has already anticipated the future in thought, in thought he has experienced it, and this experience he now recollects, instead of hoping for it. So what he hopes for lies behind him, what he recollects lies before him." See S. Crites "Storytime: Recollecting the Past and Projecting the Future" in T. R. Sarbin (ed.), *Narrative Psychology* (Praeger, 1986), pp. 152–73.
20 William Wordsworth, *Preface to the Lyrical Ballads* (1800). The 'Preface' was included in the Second Edition but not in the original publication.
21 Sarbin (ed.), *Narrative Psychology*.
22 J. Keats, 'Ode to a Grecian Urn' (1820).
23 C. G. Jung, *Analytical Psychology* (Routledge, 1978), pp. 41, 42; H. Hubert and M. Mauss, *Mélanges d'histoire des réligions* (Paris, 1909), p. xxix.
24 Keats, *op. cit.*
25 See R. Grainger, *Healing Theatre* (Trafford, 2006).
26 A. Artaud, *The Theatre and Its Double* (Calder and Boyars, 1970), p. 19.
27 *Ibid.*, p. 21.
28 "Like a business-man / investing money in a concern you suppose the spectator invests / feeling in the hero – he wants to get it back / if possible doubled." Quoted in J. Willett, *The Theatre of Bertolt Brecht* (Methuen, 1960), p. 119.
29 R. Grainger, *Healing Theatre* (Tavistock, 2006), p. 96.
30 For an extended discussion of theatrical betweenness see R. Grainger, *The Glass of Heaven* (Kingsley).
31 A. Chekhov, *Plays* (Methuen, 1988).

32 S. Beckett, *The Complete Dramatic Works* (Faber and Faber, 1986).

Four CATS AND BAGS

33 C. S. Lewis, *The Lion, the Witch and the Wardrobe* (Collins Fontana, 1980), p. 13*ff*. Although this is a story and not a play, many drama-tised versions have appeared.

34 *'Lehrstücke'* (didactic pieces) (Berlin, 1929). See J. Willett, *The Theatre of Bertolt Brecht* (Methuen, 1959/1967).

35 Shakespeare, *King Richard III* (1592). Act I, Scene 3, lines 172–83.

36 Post-Traumatic Stress is a well-documented psychological condi-tion, characterised by "intense fear, helplessness or horror . . . Trauma occurs when one loses one's sense of having a safe place to retreat within or outside oneself to deal with frightening emotions and experiences", J. L. McBride, *Spiritual Crisis: Surviving Trauma to the Soul* (Haworth Pastoral Press, 1998), p. 12. McBride's psycholog-ical sources underline the loss of security.

37 See N. Brooke, *Horrid Laughter in Jacobean Tragedy* (Barnes and Noble, 1979).

38 J. Osborne, *Look Back in Anger* (Faber and Faber, 1957), p. 28.

39 S. Beckett, *The Complete Dramatic Works* (Faber and Faber, 1986), p. 53.

40 Shakespeare, *King Henry IV, Part 2*, Act IV, Scene 5, line 42.

41 This is a reference to the production of Goldoni's *The Servant of Two Masters*, at the Swan Theatre, Stratford-on-Avon, during the late 1980s.

42 Shakespeare, *Hamlet*, Act I, Scene 2, lines 129–32.

43 *Ibid.*, Act V, Scene 1, line 279.

Five JOURNEYING

44 *The Moral Play of Everyman*, 1508–1537, lines 85–86.

45 *Ibid.,* lines 101–2.

46 Shakespeare, *Pericles, Prince of Tyre*. See R. Grainger, *Theatre and Relationship in Shakespeare's Late Plays* (Peter Lang, 2008).

47 *Ibid.*, Act V, Scene 3.

48 See R. Grainger, *The Drama of the Rite* (Sussex Academic Press, 2009).

49 D. W. Winnicott, *Playing and Reality* (Tavistock, 1971), *passim*.

50 *Ibid.*, pp. 43, 44.

51 *Ibid.*, p. 120.

Six PLOTTING

52 C. Marlowe, *Dr Faustus*, Act VI, Scene 6.

53 Bateson's phrase. 'A Theory of Play and Fantasy', in *Steps to an Ecology of Mind*, 1973).

54 See Ch. 2, n 15.

55 See Butcher, *A Commentary on Aristotle's 'Poetics'* (Dover, 1951), pp. 346*f*.

56 L. Pirandello, *Six Characters in Search of an Author* (Heinemann, 1954).

57 *Ibid.*, p. 9.

58 See W. D. Ellis, *A Sourcebook of Gestalt Psychology* (Routledge, 1938). According to Gestalt psychology, perception depends on 'closure', *i.e.* the tendency of sensations to organise themselves in recognisable wholes. Several writers are motivated with drawing attention to the mind's action in jumping ahead to the end of a series of happenings which it organizes into a meaning derived from the way the whole series fits together. R. L. Gregory, the Neurological Psychologist in *Concepts and Mechanisms of Perception* (Duckworth, 1974) describes our perceptual process itself as "Analysis-by Synthesis", and Stephen Pepper, the American Philosopher in *World Hypotheses*, (University of California, 1942), p. 233, speaks of "Contextual categories derived from the whole event". Before this, Søren Kierkegaard commented: "It is quite true what philosophers say. That life must be understood backwards. But that makes one forget the other saying that it must be lived forwards" in *The Diary of Søren Kierkegaard*, pt. 5, S. 4, entry 136; editor Peter Rohde, 1960; Citadel Press, 1998.

Seven DRAMATISING

59 "Drama is an individual pursuit undertaken within a social context . . . It is an extension of children's play, and like that play is often free and spontaneous. Drama has no fixed end product, no right or wrong way of doing. As a result, its effects, unlike theatre performances, are often unique and unrepeatable", Bernie Warren, *Drama Games* (Captus, 1989).

60 E. Goffman, *The Presentation of Self in Everyday Life* (Penguin, 1971).

61 M. M. Bakhtin, "These masks . . . grant the right to betray to the public a personal life, down to its most private and prurient little secrets" in *The Dialogic Imagination* (University of Texas Press, 1981), p. 163.

62 D. Robb (ed.), *Clowns, Fools and Picaros* (Rodopi, 2007), p. 164.

63 R. Leoncavallo, *I Pagliacci* (1892).

64 T. J., Scheff, *Goffman Unbound* (Paradigm, 2006).

65 M. M. Bakhtin, *The Dialogic Imagination*.

66 Scheff, *Goffman Unbound*, pp. viii–ix, *passim*.

Eight BELIEVING

67 T. S. Sarbin, *Narrative Psychology* (Praeger, 1986); see also D. P. McAdams, *The Stories We Live By* (Guilford 1989).
68 Personal communication, 2006.
69 See Grainger, *Healing Theatre* (2006), Ch. 8.
70 The actor concerned became a student at the Royal Academy of Dramatic Art in London when he was in his fifties, having previously been a schoolmaster in South Wales. He went on to spend the rest of his working life playing in classical theatre, mainly Shakespeare.
71 Shakespeare, *The Tempest*, Act I, Scene 2.
72 R. Grainger, 'Talking to Actors', in S. Jennings S., *Dramatherapy and Social Theatre* (Routledge, 2009), Epilogue.

Nine CONSENTING

73 S. T. Coleridge, 'The Ancient Mariner' in *Lyrical Ballads* (1798), Part I, lines 17–20.
74 V. Hugo, *Préface de Cromwell* (1827); (Paris: Classiques Larousse), p. 60.
75 See the examples cited by Mary and Kenneth Gogan, in *Social Construction: A Reader* (Sage, 2003).
76 See Chapter 3 for a discussion of this kind of theatrical sharing.
77 S. Langer, *Philosophy in a New Key: A Study in the Symbolism of Reason, Rite and Art* (New York: New American Library, 1951); see also G. Lukken, " It is characteristic of this [presentational] symbolism that it does not work in successive steps but simultaneously", *Rituals in Abundance* (Leuween: Peters, 2005), p. 29.
78 The phrase "integrating focus" comes from Edward Bailey.
79 R. Grainger, *Healing Theatre* (2006).
80 A. A. Milne, *The House at Pooh Corner* (London: Methuen, 1928), p. 127.
81 P. Berger and T. Luckman, *The Social Construction of Reality* (Harmondsworth: Penguin, 1967). The notion of "cultural reality" is widespread. The Japanese architect Toyo Ho speaks of "A virtual body . . . that has come into being through the extension of our everyday life through the media" in I. Kuhl, K. Laws, and S. Thiel-Siling, *50 Architects* (London: Prestel, 2008), p. 137.
82 F. Staal, 'The Meaninglessness of Ritual' in *Numen* 26 (1975) 1, 2–22; see also G. Lukken, *Rituals in Abundance*, pp. 39. 40.
83 *Ibid.*, p. 57.
84 The same principle – that of the unexpected reversal of expectations

– characterizes drama of all kinds, comedy and farce as well as romance and tragedy, on combinations of these categories. Whether we are surprised by something happening or not happening, what makes it dramatic is the expectation of surprises, whether or not they turn out to be justified.

85 Dramatherapy as such depends on our enactment of experience which is not our own in order that it may become ours. See S. S. Jennings (ed.), vols. 1 & 2 (1992, 1997); Jenkyns (1996); S. Pitruzzella (2004); R. Grainger (2006); D. Langley (2006); P. Jones (2007). See also R. Grimes, "Ritual gestures deeply embraced have concrete psychological results" in *Deeply Into the Bone: Reinventing Rites of Passage* (2000), p. 54.

86 *Henry VIII*. Prologue, Lines 7–9.

CONCLUSION

87 Personal communication, 2009.

BIBLIOGRAPHY

Artaud, A. (1970) *The Theatre and Its Double*. London: Calder and Boyars.

Bakhtin, M. M. (1981) *The Dialogic Imagination*. Austin: University of Texas Press.

Bateson, G. (1973) *Steps to an Ecology of Mind*. London: Paladin.

Beckett, S. (1986) *The Complete Dramatic Works*. London: Faber and Faber.

Berger, P. and Luckman, T. (1967) *The Social Construction of Reality*. Harmondsworth: Penguin.

Broadbent, D. E. (1964) *Behaviour*. London: Methuen.

Brooke, N. (1979) *Horrid Laughter in Jacobean Tragedy*. London: Barnes and Noble.

Brooke, P. (1968) *The Empty Space*. London: MacGibben and Kee.

Buber, M. (1957) *Pointing the Way*. London: Routledge.

Buber, M. (1961) *Between Man and Man*. London: Collins.

Buber, M. (1966) *I and Thou*. Edinburgh: T & T Clark.

Butcher, S. H. (1951) *A Commentary on Aristotle's 'Poetics'*. New York: Dover.

Coleridge, S. T. (1798) *Lyric Ballads*. London 1798 (with William Wordsworth).

Coleridge, S. T. (1817) *Biographia Litteraria*. London.

Duggan, M. and Grainger R. (1997) *Imagination, Identification and Catharsis in Theatre and Therapy*. London: Kingsley.

Ellis, W. D. (1938) *A Sourcebook of Gestalt Psychology*. London: Routledge.

Freud, S. (1949) *An Outline of Psychoanalysis*. London: Hogarth Press, Institute of Psychoanalysis.

Gersie, A. and King, N. (1990) *Storymaking in Education and Therapy*. London: Kingsley.

Goffman, E. (1971) *The Presentation of Self in Everyday Life*. Harmondsworth: Penguin.

Grainger, R. (1998) *The Glass of Heaven*. London: Kingsley.

Grainger, R. (2006) *Healing Theatre*. Victoria, B.C.: Trafford.

Grainger, R. (2008) *Theatre and Relationship in Shakespeare's Late Plays*. Bern: Peter Lang.

Grainger, R. (2009) *The Drama of the Rite*. Eastbourne & Portland: Sussex Academic Press.

Gregory, R. F. (1974) *Concepts and Mechanisms of Perception*. London: Duckworth.

Grimes, R. (2000) *Deeply into the Bone.* Berkeley: University of California Press.

Hubert, H. and Mauss, M. (1909) *Mélanges d'histoire des réligions.* Paris.

Hugo, V. (1827) *Préface de Cromwell.* Paris: Classiques Larousse (undated).

Jenkyns, M. (1996) *The Play's the Thing.* London: Routledge.

Jennings, S. (ed.) (1992) *Dramatherapy, Theory and Practice, Vol. 2.* London: Routledge.

Jennings, S. (ed.) (1997) *Dramatherapy, Theory and Practice, Vol. 3.* London: Routledge.

Jennings, S. (2009) *Dramatherapy and Social Theatre.* London: Routledge.

Jones, P. (2007) *Drama as Therapy.* London: Routledge.

Jung, C. G. (1978) *Analytical Psychology.* London: Routledge.

Kierkegaard, S. (1944) *Either/Or.* Cambridge, MA: Princeton University Press.

Kuhl, I., Laws, R. and Thiel-Siling, S. (2008) *50 Architects.* London: Prestel.

Laing, R. D. (1965) *The Divided Self.* Harmondsworth: Penguin.

Langer, S. (1951) *Philosophy in a New Key.* New York: New American Library.

Langley, D. (2006) *An Introduction to Dramatherapy.* London: Sage.

Lewis, C. S. (1980) *The Lion, the Witch and the Wardrobe.* London: Collins.

Lukken, G. (2005) *Rituals in Abundance.* Leuwen: Peters.

McAdams, D. P. (1989) *The Stories We Live By.* New York: Guilford.

McBride, J. L. (1998) *Spiritual Crisis: Surviving Trauma to the Soul.* New York: Haworth Pastoral Press. .

Milne A. A. (1928) *The House at Pooh Corner.* London: Methuen.

Osborne, J. (1957) *Look Back in Anger.* London: Faber and Faber.

Pepper, S. C. (1942) *World Hypotheses.* Berkeley: University of California Press.

Pirandello, L. (1954) *Six Characters in Search of an Author.* London: Heinemann.

Pitruzzella, S. (2006) *Introduction to Dramatherapy: Person and Threshold.* London: Brunner-Routledge.

Robb, D. (ed) *Clowns, Fools and Picaros.* Rodopi.

Rohde, P. (ed.) (1998) *The Diary of Sören Kierkegaard,* London: Citadel Press.

Scheff, T. S. (1979) *Catharsis in Healing, Ritual and Drama,* Berkeley, California: University of California Press.

Scheff, T. S. (2006) *Goffman Unbound.* Boulder, Colorado: Paradigm.

Sarbin. T. R. (ed.) (1986) *Narrative Psychology.* New York: Praeger.

Warren, B. (1989) *Drama Games.* London: Captus.

Willett, J. (1960) *The Theatre of Bertolt Brecht.* London: Methuen.

Winnicott, D. W. (1971) *Playing and Reality.* London: Tavistock.

INDEX